FORTIFY

Being Rooted in God's Plan for Work and Business

JASON DAVIS

With Love,

Jam N. Din

CONTENTS

Beyond The Book Media, LLC,
5174 McGinnis Ferry Rd. Suite 152
Alpharetta, GA 30005
www.beyondthebookmedia.com

The publisher is not responsible for websites that are not owned by the publisher. ISBN 978-1-953788-01-6 (Printed)

I would like to dedicate this book to my Lord and Savior, Jesus Christ. I am nothing without Him, and He gets all the glory and honor for giving me the talent and endurance to write this labor of love. To my wife, Desola, you are my queen and best friend. I love you. Thank you for your support and encouragement. To all of my family, thank you for the prayers. Many of us are called to minister in some fashion. This is my God-given way of doing so.

ACKNOWLEDGMENTS

I would like to thank Chanel E. Martin and Beyond The Book Media. You all are wonderful. Keep doing God's work in publishing. To Pastor Jordan Sharrett, Michael Blue, and Boyd Bailey: thank you for your advice and wisdom on how to properly use God's Word in the right context of Faith and Work.

FORTIFY

THE PURPOSE OF WORK

" THE LORD GOD TOOK THE MAN AND PUT HIM IN THE GARDEN OF EDEN TO WORK IT AND KEEP IT."

— GENESIS 2:15

"GOD'S WORD IS THE ROCK UPON WHICH A BUSINESS MUST BE BUILT."

— LARRY BURKETT

WORK IS FOR THE GLORY OF GOD

The word "work" can mean different things to different people. Our experiences and backgrounds play a significant role in shaping our perspective of work. What if I told you that the God of the universe cares about how you perceive work? What if there is more to work than just collecting a paycheck or providing for your family? Making a living is just one outcome of work. God views work as a process. A process of perfecting us to be more like Him. We were created in God's image to worship

Him. Our work, and the attitude with which we work, glorifies God the Father. However, what keeps us from working for the glory of God is a tainted view of work.

A TAINTED VIEW

The concepts of work and business are perhaps some of the most misconstrued words in the dictionary. Some people view these as something they merely do. Necessary events purely to pay the bills and meet daily needs. Others view them as drudgery. An arduous process that comes with a negative connotation and requires stressful effort. Then there are those who attach their identity to these terms. With almost an unnatural obsession, they have trouble reconciling their responsibilities between the office and home.

If you are honest with yourself, you've probably had one of the above thoughts floating around in your head at some point. I know I have. We develop these paradigms of work and business for two primary reasons: the influence of others and the influence of self. Relying on the influence of others for a proper outlook of work can be problematic. This can be seen through the concept of the "sacred cow."

First and foremost, what is a "sacred cow?" Sacred cows are unchanging, idolized processes we use in business. Whenever you hear employees or a company use verbiage like "that's just how we do things" or "we've always done it this way," look out! An organization that subjects itself to abiding by "sacred cow thinking" misses out on opportunities for innovation and continuous improvement. Because of the potential missteps of the "sacred cow," it can lead to insanity. The working definition of insanity I'm using, in this case, is doing the same thing over and over again and expecting different results.

Relying on the influence of self for an outlook of work can also be problematic. Human beings are creatures, creatures of habit that is. One very poor habit we have is ignorance. Now there are two kinds of ignorance: pure ignorance and willful ignorance. Pure ignorance is the essence of simply not knowing. Willful ignorance is knowing but refusing to act on prior knowledge. The primary issue with "ignoring" wise counsel and doing what we want is that it's rooted in pride. Proverbs 16:18 says, "Pride goes before destruction, and a haughty spirit before a fall." If we're not careful, we can arrogantly form opinions about work and business that take us down a road of darkness.

Let's venture a little bit deeper. Why does the concept of work so often get associated with a negative connotation? We must time travel back to the garden of Eden.

Genesis 3:17-19 "And to Adam he said, 'Because you have listened to the voice of your wife and have eaten of the tree of which I commanded you, 'You shall not eat of it,' cursed is the ground because of you; in pain you shall eat of it all the days of your life; thorns and thistles it shall bring forth for you; and you shall eat the plants of the field. By the sweat of your face you shall eat bread, till you return to the ground, for out of it you were taken; for you are dust, and to dust you shall return.'"

The fall of mankind happened through Adam and Eve's sin. The ground becoming cursed and toil by the sweat of our faces became lasting consequences we still experience today as a result. Sin entering the world set off an enormous chain reaction for work and business. Notice the Bible says that "cursed is the ground because of you..." Adam and Eve lost privileges from living in the garden of Eden, but mankind itself was not cursed. The ground was. To yield a harvest of any kind, whether it's the cultivation of crops or a new startup venture, it's going to take hard work.

Over several thousand years, the amount of discipline it took to labor for a profit became painful for the human race. Work and business began to take on a disposition of "work as drudgery." Work is a call from God to serve others, and a work as drudgery mindset is inconsistent with God's view of work. Sin infected the marketplace with awful symptoms such as laziness, selfishness, jealousy, get rich quick schemes, political maneuvering, and worst of all, greed.

The disease state of modern-day business is rooted in two destructive traits: pride and fear. Pride was the first sin exhibited by the angel Lucifer, who would later become Satan. It resulted in his ousting from Heaven. See Isaiah 14:12-14.

"How you are fallen from heaven, O Day Star, son of Dawn! How you are cut down to the ground, you who laid the nations low! You said in your heart, 'I will ascend to heaven; above the stars of God I will set my throne on high; I will sit on the mount of assembly in the far reaches of the north; I will ascend above the heights of the clouds; I will make myself like the Most High.'

Pride elevates *me* and puts down *we*. Pride promotes selfishness over generosity. Pride demands more at all costs. Pride, however, has very clear consequences highlighted throughout the Bible.

Fear is the toxic fallout from sin back in the Garden of Eden. After Adam and Eve ate the fruit, God called out to Adam, looking for them. They had a fearful reaction. See Genesis 3:8-11.

"And they heard the sound of the Lord God walking in the garden in the cool of the day, and the man and his wife hid themselves from the presence of the Lord God among the trees of the garden. But the Lord God called to the man and said to him, 'Where are you?' And he said, 'I heard the sound of you in the garden, and I was afraid, because I was naked, and I hid myself.' He said, 'Who told you that you were naked? Have you eaten of the tree of which I commanded you not to eat?'"

Fear is the gateway to irrational behavior. Fear blinds us from reality and cripples our progress.

The deadly combination of pride and fear has created a spiritual paradigm of scarcity in the marketplace. Pride and fear are merely acknowledgments of a lack of faith in God's ability to provide. Our father of faith, Abraham, declared God's supreme provision in Genesis 22:14.

"So, Abraham called the name of that place, "The Lord will provide"; as it is said to this day, "On the mount of the Lord it shall be provided."

Business can be cutthroat and lonely at times. But followers of Christ are never alone, even when we feel like we are. God gives us this promise in Deuteronomy 31:6.

"Be strong and courageous. Do not fear or be in dread of them, for it is the Lord your God who goes with you. He will not leave you or forsake you."

Though resources on Earth can at times be difficult to obtain, God's economy is one of abundance. In our weaknesses (this includes shortcomings in business), He is strong. See 2 Corinthians 12:10.

"For the sake of Christ, then, I am content with weaknesses, insults, hardships, persecutions, and calamities. For when I am weak, then I am strong."

A PROPER VIEW

Humans are deeply flawed individuals in need of a savior. Enter Jesus Christ. So why do we selfishly believe that we have the power and authority to dictate the purpose of work and business? The answer is we don't. The only person worthy of giving a proper mandate on work and business is God the Father. You might be thinking to yourself, *did God actually give a mandate for work?* He did. Let's explore this mandate in Genesis 1:28.

> And God blessed them. And God said to them, "Be fruitful and multiply and fill the earth and subdue it, and have dominion over the fish of the sea and over the birds of the heavens and over every living thing that moves on the earth."

Scholars refer to this mandate from God as the "Cultural

Mandate" or "Creation Mandate."[1] Pay very close attention. There are some extremely powerful concepts that set up God's purpose for man, the earth, and the concept of work. The order of how this scripture is written is not by coincidence. Before God commands mankind, He blesses them! Pause for a second. The God of the universe gave forth blessing before He gave us instruction! Our heavenly Father loves us deeply and passionately. God is good and gives good gifts. James 1:17 says, "Every good gift and every perfect gift is from above, coming down from the Father of lights, with whom there is no variation or shadow due to change."

God then follows up the blessing with a command: "Be fruitful and multiply..." Let's talk about the significance of the words *fruitful* and *multiply*. In order to understand their significance, we must understand their meaning. Dictionary.com defines fruitful as "producing good results; beneficial; profitable:"[2] This is God's call for procreation, that men and women have children.

A fruitful entity is one that yields a good return of fruit. Jesus Christ talks about bearing fruit in John 15:5. "I am the vine; you are the branches. Whoever abides in me and I in him, he it is that bears much fruit, for apart from me you can do nothing." Whether it be the fruit of procreation (Genesis 1:28) or the fruit of the Spirit that Jesus references in John 15, fruitfulness comes from God.

If we're called to be fruitful (effective) and bear fruit, we must be connected to the Source. The good news is that we were connected to the Source from the beginning! When man fell out of fellowship with God through sin, we became disconnected from the Source. Jesus' sacrifice on the cross once again gave us access to the Source by saving our souls by grace through faith. Our ability to be effective doesn't exist without Jesus. Apart from Jesus, we are branches that wither away.

In our being fruitful, what kind of fruit are we to bear? The apostle Paul tells us in Galatians 5:22-23, "But the fruit of the

Spirit is love, joy, peace, patience, kindness, goodness, faithfulness, gentleness, self-control; against such things there is no law." Paul interestingly admonishes us about the works of the flesh just prior to giving the fruit of the Spirit in Galatians 5:19-21. "Now the works of the flesh are evident: sexual immorality, impurity, sensuality, idolatry, sorcery, enmity, strife, jealousy, fits of anger, rivalries, dissensions, divisions, envy, drunkenness, orgies, and things like these. I warn you, as I warned you before, that those who do such things will not inherit the kingdom of God."

Whether you're an entrepreneur or an employee, you've more than likely seen versions of the spiritual fruit and fleshly works lived out in the workplace. When you compare the works of the flesh with the fruit of the Spirit, you can easily see why they conflict with each other. The fruit produced by our effectiveness (fruitful) should bring a harvest of the Spirit, not the sinful flesh. The flesh, whose wages produce death, prevent multiplication from going forth.

Dictionary.com defines multiply as "to grow in number, quantity, etc.; increase."[3] Multiplication is multidimensional and does go beyond reproduction. Make no mistake, family is a fundamental part of God's plan. He began the world in a triune relationship (with Jesus and the Holy Spirit). See the keywords *us* and *our* in Genesis 1:26. "Then God said, "Let **us** make man in **our** image, after **our** likeness. And let them have dominion over the fish of the sea and over the birds of the heavens and over the livestock and over all the earth and over every creeping thing that creeps on the earth."

Taking a closer look at Genesis 1:26, we also see that we are made in God's "image" and "likeness." By this point in scripture, God had already designed, organized, classified, and blessed the Earth and everything in it. Multiplication involves man increasing in these same characteristics and attributes. The main difference being, God creates from nothing whereas man creates from something. When you put together the phrase of scripture

"Be fruitful and multiply" from Genesis 1:28, another way of saying this is **"To be effective and grow."**

If we are to be effective and grow, how do we go about doing that? Let's take another look at Genesis 1:28. "...and fill the earth and subdue it," The definition of *fill* is "to make full. To abound or overflow." God commissioned man to make the Earth abound! Let's keep going. Take a look at the word "subdue." According to Wayne Grudem, the word *subdue*, which is derived from the Hebrew word *kabash*, implies making use of the Earth's resources."[4] In other words, cultivation or the concept of productivity. When we work, it's is an opportunity for us to honor God, use the gifts He's bestowed upon us, and flourish as a community of people. God wants us to use the Earth's resources for His glory! By using the Earth's resources for the glory of God, that's how we effectively grow society and civilization.

Productivity from the beginning was blessed and initiated by God. God desired someone to work the Earth. God called man to do so. See Genesis 2:5-8 and Genesis 2:15.

"When no bush of the field was yet in the land and no small plant of the field had yet sprung up—for the Lord God had not caused it to rain on the land, and there was no man to work the ground, and a mist was going up from the land and was watering the whole face of the ground—then the Lord God formed the man of dust from the ground and breathed into his nostrils the breath of life, and the man became a living creature. And the Lord God planted a garden in Eden, in the east, and there he put the man whom he had formed."

— GENESIS 2:5-8

Genesis 2:15 says, "The Lord God took the man and put him in the garden of Eden to work it and keep it."

Adam's first responsibilities were working the garden,

keeping the garden, and naming the animals. This is significant because Adam's responsibilities were the first recorded human jobs. A gardener and administrator. God's job description is Creator and Master Designer. If you look at the workplace today, you can see these same attributes from God and Adam. I hope you are beginning to see the significance of work and business. It's all part of God's plan.

WORK SERVES THE GREATER GOOD

God is good all the time. And all the time, God is good. A good God produces good things. Skillful work, conducted in the confines of business, serves the greater good. God the Father is a relational God. He exists in a trinity (Father, Son, Holy Ghost). What if we looked at business as a way to build community with God and with each other? The skills, gifts, and talents we've all been blessed with offer tremendous value to others. In other words, we've been blessed to be a blessing. Consider the satisfaction one has when providing an excellent product or service to make an impactful contribution to society.

What does building community with God look like? It looks a lot like what Adam and Eve experienced in the Garden of Eden. They walked directly with God and spoke to Him daily. Imagine working for and with the God of the universe face to face! Certainly, a glorious and majestic site it must have been. What does building community with each other look like? It looks like working and meeting the marketplace needs of each other in love. No pretense. No greed. No hidden agenda. Simply conducting business for the glory of God and putting agape love on display. There's another term in business that communicates tight-knit association with one another: partnership.

ELEVATING PARTNERSHIP

The power of agreement (partnership) is one of the most robust gifts of faith that God has ever created. It's a principle that far transcends everyday circumstances. Let's take a look at an example in scripture where an unlikely union exhibited the power of agreement.

The Tower of Babel - Genesis 11:6 "And the Lord said, "Behold, they are one people, and they have all one language, and this is only the beginning of what they will do. And nothing that they propose to do will now be impossible for them."

Wow. The people of Earth put their minds together to build an imposing structure to the heavens. They had the wrong intentions (see Genesis 11:3-4), yet their partnership transcended even their moral compass. God saw His principle of agreement in action and knew He had to do something about it because there was no end to their ambition (see Genesis 11:7-9).

In the same way, we see all kinds of innovation and technological breakthroughs occur in the marketplace by way of partnership. There are two patterns in particular which partnership has yielded fruit in business: "partnership by entity" and "partnership by people."

Our working definition of "partnership by entity" simply means two organizations associating together to collaborate on a product or service. Here is a short list of some prominent co-branded product launches:

- Apple/Goldman-Sachs – Apple Card
- Samsung/Google – Samsung Galaxy Phone Series
- Disney/Comcast – Hulu
- Verizon/Vodafone – Mobile Wireless Network

Our working definition of "partnership by people" means two individuals collaborating to build, found, and/or deliver a product or service. Here is a short list of some prominent business pairs/duos:

- Steve Jobs/Steve Wozniak – Apple
- Bill Gates/Paul Allen – Microsoft
- Ben Cohen/Jerry Greenfield – Ben & Jerry's
- Richard L. Simon/M. Lincoln Schuster – Simon & Schuster
- Richard McDonald/Maurice McDonald – McDonald's

As we can see, the power of partnership (agreement) has produced incredible business successes that individuals couldn't dream of doing on their own. Proverbs 27:17 says, "Iron sharpens iron, and one man sharpens another." Ecclesiastes 4:9 says, "Two are better than one, because they have a good reward for their toil." Where one entity or person is weak, another excels in. **Business glorifies God in a spirit of unity.**

THE PROCESS NOT THE PROJECT

Profit, revenue, sales, positive cash flow, and increased market share are all outcomes that businesses seek. And they should if they want to stay in business. But I'd like to submit for your consideration another perspective. What if God wants more out of our work than just earthly success criteria? If you shatter sales records and profit margins but lose yourself along the way, what good is that? Jesus asked that very question in Mark 8:36. "For what does it profit a man to gain the whole world and forfeit his soul?" God cares about the perfection and production of your character. And ladies and gentlemen, the shaping of your character is most definitely a process.

God wants us to embrace the process, not the project or target in progress (whatever it may be). We seem to quickly forget that God controls the outcome. If God wants your sales to spike, He'll do it. If He wants them to plummet, He'll do it.

He wants you to learn lessons along the way so that you become more Christ-like. Remember, if we call ourselves Christians, "Christ" is the root word.

Work is more complex than it's ever been because businesses are setting out to solve more complex problems in the market-place. The day to day grind of work can produce weariness, fatigue, and a lack of faith if we're not careful. Take the story of Noah, for instance. He built an ark that took years for a weather pattern that had never existed before. When God finally sent the rain, Noah was 600 years old! Years of manual labor, 40 days of flooding, and 150 days of floating at sea. Weariness was an understatement. But God blessed Noah because of his faithfulness, devotion, and obedience.

There are tons of other scriptures that speak of the sanctification (maturation) process.

Hebrews 12:11: "For the moment all discipline seems painful rather than pleasant, but later it yields the peaceful fruit of righteousness to those who have been trained by it."

James 1:2-4: "Count it all joy, my brothers, when you meet trials of various kinds, for you know that the testing of your faith produces steadfastness. And let steadfastness have its full effect, that you may be perfect and complete, lacking in nothing."

Romans 8:18: "For I consider that the sufferings of this present time are not worth comparing with the glory that is to be revealed to us."

The maturation process is timely and strategic. For example, think about how wine is made. Before you get to the sweet, smooth, or earthy taste you know and love, clusters of grapes first had to be picked. The season in which the grapes were grown and the kind of soil they were cultivated in points to timeliness. The crushing, fermentation, and temperature in which the grapes are aged in points to specificity.

What you do (vocation) matters to God, but how you go about it (sanctification journey) matters even more to God.

CHAPTER TAKEAWAYS

1. What keeps us from working for the glory of God is a tainted view of work.
2. If we're not careful, we can arrogantly form opinions about work and business that take us down a road of darkness.
3. Business glorifies God in a spirit of unity.

EMBODY STEWARDSHIP

" FOR IT WILL BE LIKE A MAN GOING ON A JOURNEY, WHO CALLED HIS SERVANTS AND ENTRUSTED TO THEM HIS PROPERTY."

— MATTHEW 25:14

"STEWARDSHIP IS THE ESSENCE OF FAITHFULLY MANAGING THE RESOURCES YOU'VE BEEN ENTRUSTED WITH."

— JASON DAVIS

GOD IS THE OWNER

I believe that many Christians *know* God is in charge and yet, at the same time, fail to acknowledge that God *is* in charge. Knowing something with your head is surface level. Knowing something in your heart is core level. This spiritual vs. mental acknowledgment sets up a very real rivalry that occurs daily, especially in the business world. The problem is this rivalry is futile because God has no rival or equal. Throughout scripture,

God reveals Himself through different titles to demonstrate His mighty presence and glory.

Isaiah 9:6 (partial) says, "...his name shall be called **Wonderful Counselor, Mighty God, Everlasting Father, Prince of Peace.**"

In John 14:6, Jesus said to him, "I am **the way**, and **the truth**, and **the life**. No one comes to the Father except through me."

Revelation 1:8 says, "I am **the Alpha** and **the Omega**, says the Lord God, "who is and who was and who is to come, **the Almighty**."

As you can see, the impact, grandeur, and sovereignty of The Father, Son, and Holy Spirit is made quite clear in scripture. But one area of supremacy that isn't taught on nearly enough is God as "The Owner." In Matthew 25:14, Jesus tells a story called The Parable of the Talents. There is a pivotal part at the beginning of the story that sets the tone: "For it will be like a man (Jesus) going on a journey, **who called his servants (us) and entrusted to them (us) his (Jesus') property**." Don't miss this. We are called servants of God to take care of the resources (businesses, ideas, properties, etc.) He allocates to us. This allocation or entrusting process is what is known as stewardship. Stewardship is the essence of faithfully managing the resources you've been entrusted with. God is the owner, and we are His managers (stewards).

GOD OWNS IT ALL

We've elaborated above on the nature of God as owner. But what does He being the owner look like in form? We know that God is the Creator of the Heavens and Earth. As Creator, He also owns all of the resources and rights that come with His creation. Let's examine God's ownership of the world's resources.

Deuteronomy 10:14 says, "Behold, to the Lord your God

belong heaven and the heaven of heavens, the earth with all that is in it."

Psalm 24:1 states, "The earth is the Lord's and the fullness thereof, the world and those who dwell therein,"

Haggai 2:8 says, "The silver is mine, and the gold is mine, declares the Lord of hosts."

Psalm 50:10-11 says, "For every beast of the forest is mine, the cattle on a thousand hills. I know all the birds of the hills, and all that moves in the field is mine."

God, the owner, exists outside of the world's economy. He's a God of abundance, not scarcity. It's important to honor God in all that we do in business and work so that we keep the right perspective. The right perspective being, we own nothing and only manage that which has been given to us.

God as the owner also means He holds the money bag. Think of Him as the "Ultimate Banker." He knows the intent of our hearts and how we go about pursuing compensation in the marketplace. Unlike society's success criteria, God has His own, which is countercultural. There are three principles God gives us to have the opportunity for success. The keyword is *opportunity*.

1. **Seek first God's kingdom and righteousness** – Matthew 6:33 says, "But seek first the kingdom of God and his righteousness, and all these things will be added to you."
2. **Be willing and obedient** – Isaiah 1:19 says, "If you are willing and obedient, you shall eat the good of the land."
3. **Trust God** – Proverbs 3:5-6 says, "Trust in the Lord with all your heart, and do not lean on your own understanding. In all your ways acknowledge him, and he will make straight your paths."

THE ULTIMATE STEWARD

God is not only the gracious owner, but He's also a faithful steward himself. In fact, he's the ultimate steward. So much so, that He divided His responsibilities across a trinity. Now stay with me. I know it seems strange for someone to assign themselves multiple jobs, but this is the case. God is one unit consisting of three persons: God The Father, Jesus Christ The Son, and The Holy Spirit. They each have their own roles. God's wisdom is infinite and cannot be comprehended by men. I do not claim to know how God chooses to reveal Himself through each role. Three examples in the book of 2 Corinthians display God relationally.

2 Corinthians 13:14 states, "The grace of the Lord Jesus Christ and the love of God and the fellowship of the Holy Spirit be with you all."

The Love Giver (God The Father) – the "love of God."

The Grace Giver (Jesus Christ The Son) – the "grace of the Lord Jesus Christ."

The Fellowship Giver (The Holy Spirit) – the "fellowship of the Holy Spirit."

God the owner walks His talk. God follows His own lead. God is the author and finisher of our faith.

WE ARE MANAGERS

We broke down the definition of stewardship earlier. Now let us explore the individual who has entered into this operation of faithful management and administration: the steward. According to Dictionary.com, a steward is "a person who manages another's property or financial affairs; one who administers anything as the agent of another or others."[5] Stewardship is an evolving process, much like the ongoing nature of nurturing and building a friendship or relationship. In the same way, stewards are on a journey; they do seek to arrive at a final destination. Stewards are running a marathon, not a sprint. There are three essential values a steward must learn while in the process: leadership, wisdom, and discipline.

The first value is leadership. We will examine leadership more explicitly in a later chapter, but leadership plays a key role in the stewardship process. In order to manage and administer a business, product, project, or initiative well, one must obtain influence. That's where leadership comes into the picture. John Maxwell says that "leadership is influence; nothing more, nothing less."[6] Furthermore, James C. Hunter describes leadership this way in his book, *The Servant*: "...the skill of influencing people to work enthusiastically toward goals identified as being for the common good. Simply put, leadership is about getting things done through people."[7]

Once you gain influence with your team or organization, you need insight on how and when to use it. Enter the second value: wisdom. Wisdom is the proper application of knowledge. Unused knowledge is just merely information. The blueprint for running or working in a business is developing a deep dependency on God. Wisdom won't automatically come to you. You must seek it out. The best description I've seen of this seeking process for wisdom comes from the title of a daily devotional called *Wisdom Hunters* by Boyd Bailey. You must become a "hunter of wisdom." Here are four key tenets in scripture to remember about wisdom:

1. **Wisdom is paramount** – Proverbs 4:7 NLT says, "Getting wisdom is the wisest thing you can do! And whatever else you do, develop good judgment."[8]
2. **Wisdom can be freely accessed** – James 1:5 says, "If any of you lacks wisdom, let him ask God, who gives generously to all without reproach, and it will be given him."
3. **Wisdom starts with reverence** – Proverbs 9:10 states, "The fear of the Lord is the beginning of

wisdom, and the knowledge of the Holy One is
insight."

4. **Wisdom is available if you look in the right
   place** – Proverbs 1:20 says, "Wisdom cries aloud in
   the street, in the markets she raises her voice;"

Leadership sparks the flame of stewardship, but wisdom
guides the flame.

Think about how a car is powered. We'll use a vehicle
metaphor to summarize our stewardship exploration. Leadership
(influence) is what ignites stewardship. Wisdom is the insightful
GPS that escorts stewardship in the right direction. The only
element we haven't talked about is gas. Discipline, our third
value, is the fuel stewardship runs on. Retired Navy SEAL
Officer Jocko Willink notes that "Discipline equals freedom."[9]
John Maxwell states in his Law of Consistency that "Motivation
gets you going, but discipline keeps you growing."[10] The tenets
outlined by both Willink and Maxwell reveal to us that discipline
fuels stewardship towards two positive outcomes: freedom and
growth. For example, financial freedom comes from one's ability
to be disciplined with budgeting. Growth also occurs in the
process because the skillset of budgeting is sharpened by repetition. The above example shows us how good habits and consistency are developed by being disciplined. Discipline helps
businesses and employees consistently deliver value to the
customer within an agreed upon service level expectation. Doing
so results in what Rabbi Daniel Lapin refers to as customers,
giving you green "certificates of performance."[11]

UNIQUE VESSELS

In Matthew 25, we see that the master (Jesus) distributes talents
to the servants (us). A talent in those times equaled a significant
amount of money. The talents were given "to each according to
his ability." God knows exactly what we as His servants can

handle and assigns accordingly. He knows our strengths, weaknesses, fears, and triumphs. We don't have to worry about a lack of ingenuity. He will lead, guide, and direct us. Whether a small business, franchise, or large national corporation, they are to be managed well by the steward.

There is no mention in scripture whether or not the servants knew each other or if they were aware of how the master was distributing the talents. This is very subtle, but we can't miss it. Don't worry about the gifts and talents given to others. We are fearfully and wonderfully made with our own unique calling. Be the best steward YOU can be. That's what the master expects. So many businesses fail because they spend too much time trying to be something they're not. Customers have a keen sense and can smell when a company isn't being authentic.

Staying with the Parable of the Talents, the servants who were given five and two talents knew their master well and wanted to get a return for him. However, the servant given the one talent dug a pit and hid his talent in the ground. Let's home in on this portion of scripture. The image the one talent servant had of the master was totally different from the five and two talent servants. He knew the master to "be a hard man."

Unfortunately, so many Christian business leaders treat God the same way. They view Him as a heartless taskmaster. This is far from the truth. Jesus said that "My yoke is easy, and my burden is light." Jesus IS the truth and spoke the truth in love. Abiding in the truth (Jesus) also means receiving the grace of God. Jesus stands at the door of man's heart and knocks steadfastly. Mankind must take a step of faith and receive God's grace. When you truly accept the grace and goodness of God, you act more like the five and two talent servants, not the "wicked and lazy" servant who squandered his talent.

When we manage our businesses and occupations well, we honor God. Much greater than obtaining money is how our heavenly Father sees us. When we are good stewards over what God has entrusted to us, we afford ourselves the opportunity to manage more (see Matthew 25:14-30). There's nothing better than being commended by the master on a job well done, having your responsibility increased, and entering into the joy of the Master. As unique vessels, we take our gifts and talents and carry innovation, creativity, and problem solving into the world economy.

MARKETPLACE AMBASSADORS

Have you ever heard the phrase "put on your Sunday Best?" I used to hear this all the time growing up in church. The phrase signified putting your best foot forward (and attire) to worship the Lord on Sunday. There's nothing wrong with getting excited about what God is going to do at church on Sunday. We should have the attitude David describes in Psalm 100:4. "Enter his gates with thanksgiving, and his courts with praise! Give thanks to him; bless his name!" I would, however, like to bring attention to a sad trend that's permeated the hearts and minds of Christians upon leaving Church on Sundays.

We don't have that same fire in our souls Monday through Saturday. We don't have that same spirit of thanksgiving and praise elevated on weekdays. Yes, many churches have some kind of mid-week Bible Study. But the emphasis just isn't the same as Sunday. What's worse is that we take this same lack of fire into our jobs and places of work. Why is this such a big deal? Work is where the majority of us spend our time during the week.

According to the Bureau of Labor Statistics, Americans work an average of 34.4 hours per week.[12] For all the emphasis put on Sundays, what's more staggering is that overall church membership has declined sharply since the 1930s.[13] That's a lot of time away from family and not at church. I'm not going after what's wrong with churches. For more on that topic, you might want to check out North Point Community Church Pastor Andy Stanley's book, *Irresistible*. There are spiritual leaders God is raising up to bring people back into the church. What I am going after is this: what's preventing YOU from sharing the gospel of Jesus Christ at your place of work?

The workplace is absolutely where the non-believer is, but we act like God isn't with us on the weekly morning commute to work. Authors Dave Spada and Dave Scott refer to this demeanor as being a "Monday Morning Atheist." A "Monday Morning Atheist" is someone who believes in God but works like He doesn't exist.[14] If we're honest, we've all found ourselves in this position before. Let me tell you a quick story about how God permanently changed my focus at work.

One day after coming out of a meeting, I was very disgruntled about one of my co-workers. This particular person was difficult to deal with. I found myself complaining about this individual under my breath for about 10-15 minutes. While walking in the hallway alone, an audible voice spoke to me. It was the Holy Spirit. He asked, "Jason, why don't you stop complaining about people and find a way to encourage them instead?" Ouch. Gut punch to the heart. But this led me to look to God's Word for what it says about encouraging people. God introduced me to Hebrews 3:13, and I've never been the same since. Hebrews 3:13 AMP says, "But continually encourage one another every day, as long as it is called "Today" [and there is an opportunity] so that none of you will be hardened [into settled rebellion] by the deceitfulness of sin [its cleverness, delusive glamour, and sophistication]."[15] I now speak life into the office. I now pray for my co-workers. I find a way to sprinkle scripture into conversations and presentations. I do whatever I can to inject the encouraging presence of God into the market.

Encouraging others brings us in alignment with being mission-driven. Ladies and gentlemen, as stewards, we are called to manage the mission that God gave us. If you've ever wondered what your life's purpose is, listen up. God gave all of us a three-part mission.

1. **Love God** – Mark 12:30 says, "And you shall **love the**

Lord your God with all your heart and with all your soul and with all your mind and with all your strength."

2. **Love People** – Mark 12:31 says, "The second is this: 'You shall **love your neighbor** as yourself."

3. **Make Disciples** – Matthew 28:19 says, "Go therefore and **make disciples** of all nations, baptizing them in the name of the Father and of the Son and of the Holy Spirit, teaching them to observe all that I have commanded you. And behold, I am with you always, to the end of the age."

Fulfilling God's mission on the job means being a "Marketplace Ambassador." According to R. Paul Stevens, 122 out of 132 of Jesus' public appearances were in the marketplace.[16] Be Christ-like and let your light shine so people will see God's works in you and through you. They'll see your spirit of excellence and eventually come inquiring about what makes you different. Once your "salt and light" draws others into meaningful discussion, follow a simple model to lead them to Christ the way founding Perimeter Church Pastor Randy Pope recommends.[17]

GBI

G – Greet: Approach people with genuine concern and curiosity

B – Befriend: Begin to build purposeful friendships with people

I – Invite: Give people an authentic, Holy Spirit inspired invitation to hear the gospel of Jesus Christ.

GOD'S FINANCIAL PLAYBOOK

As a stewardship coach and teacher, I simply could not end this chapter without providing guidance on money management. There are over 2000 scriptures in the Bible about money and possessions. The world says a lot about money, but God says more. Whether you work at a large corporate Fortune 500 or run a small business, God's financial principles transcend any kind of business circumstance. Two major categories a business must be laser-focused on are debt and cash reserves.

First and foremost, debt is not a sin or a matter of salvation. But its handling is a matter of wisdom and integrity. Proverbs 22:7 says, "The rich rules over the poor, and the borrower is the slave of the lender." This text touches on what I call the 2 Rs: reality and relationship.

When you owe another person or entity money, there is a straightforward reality that you have entered into an agreement to repay the debt, as stated in the terms. Once the ink dries, contractually, you're expected to pay. God agrees. Psalm 37:21 says, "The wicked borrows but does not pay back, but the righteous is generous and gives;" Bottom line, if you owe a debt, pay the debt. To God, this is a matter of integrity.

Owing a person or entity creates a change in relationship, and it's not a favorable one. Specifically, the back half of Proverbs 22:7 states that having debt creates a master-slave relationship. As long as one has an outstanding balance, he or she is subject to the creditor. Before you go out and seek a loan, pray and ask God if that's the right direction to go in. You never know how God will intervene on your behalf. Leave room for God to work before taking things into your own hands.

Ron Blue tells a good story about how God intervened in his decision to borrow money. When Ron first went into business, he decided to take out a loan of around $10,000-15,000 to help cover family expenses until he could turn a profit. Within a week of taking out the loan, God spoke to Ron and told him to get rid of the line of credit. Ron obeyed.

Coca-Cola, whom Ron had prior business dealings, called him in because they liked the financial principles he taught. When the topic of compensation came up, guess what amount of money was offered to Ron for his services? The exact amount that Ron had originally taken out as a loan! Go to God before taking things into your own hands or following the status quo that everyone else does in business.[18]

The repayment of liabilities should be a priority for a business. The Bible discusses a sense of urgency to get out of debt in Proverbs 6:1-5:

> My son, if you have **put up security** for your neighbor, have given your pledge for a stranger, if you are snared in the words of your mouth, caught in the words of your mouth, then do this, my son, and save yourself, for you have come into the hand of your neighbor: **go, hasten**, and **plead urgently** with your neighbor. Give your eyes no sleep and your eyelids no slumber; save yourself like a gazelle from the hand of the hunter, like a bird from the hand of the fowler."

If you are going to borrow, there are really two main rules of thumb to consider:

1. Understand the terms of the debt you're taking on (interest rate, term, etc.)
2. You must have a guaranteed way to repay (examine budget, cash flow, streams of income, etc.).

As God blesses the works of your hands to generate revenue for your business, savings (or cash reserves) should be another business priority. The Bible talks about the wisdom associated with good saving habits in Proverbs 21:20. "Precious treasure and oil are in a wise man's dwelling, but a foolish man devours it."

This wisdom also has practicality associated with it. Joseph saved entire nations during a seven-year famine (modern-day called a recession) because he heeded the lesson from Proverbs 21:20. During years of plenty, or what we would call a thriving economy, he exercised prudence by putting away 20% of the nation's grain (income).

Genesis 41:33-40:

Now therefore let Pharaoh select a discerning and wise man, and set him over the land of Egypt. Let Pharaoh proceed to appoint overseers over the land and take one-fifth of the produce of the land of Egypt during the seven plentiful years. And let them gather all the food of these good years that are coming and store up grain under the authority of Pharaoh for food in the cities, and let them keep it. That food shall be a reserve for the land against the seven years of famine that are to occur in the land of Egypt, so that the land may not perish through the famine. This proposal pleased Pharaoh and all his servants. And Pharaoh said to his servants, "Can we find a man like this, in whom is the Spirit of God?" Then Pharaoh said to Joseph, "Since God has shown you all this, there is none so discerning and wise as you are. You shall be over my house, and all my people shall order themselves as you command. Only as regards the throne will I be greater than you."

At the time of this writing, the fallout from the coronavirus (COVID-19) is affecting thousands of businesses worldwide. This pandemic has exposed the necessity of emergency savings for the marketplace. If you've lived through The Great Recession (2007-2009) or The Stock Market Crash of 1987, then you certainly understand how important this is. Don't conform to the world's way of handling business finances; transform the health of your business by handling money God's way. Let me also say this: if you work in the capacity of a C-Level executive

(CEO, CFO, COO, etc.) or a board member at a large institution, speak up and find a way to influence the trajectory of the organization by instilling God's financial principles. Remember, principles transcend circumstances.

If you are looking for a more streamlined way of keeping the books for your business, I recommend Mike Michalowicz's book *Profit First*. Mike is very transparent about the position he put himself in financially by not being a good steward of his business. This brings up another point that I've seen many business owners and entrepreneurs struggle with. Both your business and personal finances should be managed with excellence. If you make 2 million dollars annually but are overwhelmed with debt and spend your money frivolously, that does not demonstrate good stewardship. Likewise, if your personal finances are in order, but you're running the business into the ground financially, that also isn't good stewardship. God expects HIS money, whether consumer or business, to be managed for HIS glory.

Three of the best principles I've heard to guide your personal finances came from Art Rainer's book, *The Money Challenge*. The three principles are to Give Generously, Save Wisely, and Live Appropriately.[19]

Generosity needs to be at the core of our finances. Giving should be prioritized, systematic, proportional to income, and done with the right attitude. We see these concepts in scripture.

Prioritized: Proverbs 3:9-10 – "Honor the LORD with your wealth and with the **firstfruits** of all your produce; then your barns will be filled with plenty, and your vats will be bursting with wine."

Systematic/Proportional To Income: 1 Corinthians 16:2 – "On the **first day of the week**, each of you is to put something aside and store it up, **as he may prosper**, so that there will be no collecting when I come."

The Right Attitude: 2 Corinthians 9:7 – "Each one must give as he has **decided in his heart**, not reluctantly or under compulsion, for God loves a **cheerful giver**."

Prioritizing giving means it is the first expenditure to come out of your income before other household expenses, lest you start rationalizing and negotiating what else to do with your money. Systematic giving could look like setting up a recurring or automated amount per month for your church and other non-profit institutions. Proportional giving sets up the practice of increasing your giving as your income increases. The right attitude towards giving is one that's motivated by love and gratitude, not by what reward you will get as a tax benefit. Probably the most hotly debated Christian financial topic on giving is how much we should give. To answer that, we need to understand two things: 1) We are now under grace, not the law. When Jesus died on the cross and rose again, He fulfilled the law and everything that came with it. 2) The Law of the Tithe is different from The Principle of the Tithe.

First off, tithe literally means "a tenth." Any amount below or above ten percent is an offering. The Law of the Tithe is what Malachi 3:6-12 references. The Principle of Tithe was initiated by Abraham when he gave the King and High Priest Melchizedek ten percent of his wealth (Genesis 14:17-20). This is important because Abraham lived hundreds of years before God gave the law through Moses. Meaning, Abraham had no standard or rule to follow. He simply gave because he was thankful.

We are free to "give what's purposed in our heart." The tithe (10%) is a great amount to start your giving with because it's mathematically simple to derive from a budgeting perspective. If you can't start with the tithe, start with what you have. Whether it's $20 a month or 5% of your income, just get started. But wherever you start, don't remain where you are. If you're already giving the tithe, what would it take for you to give a little more? Whether you're currently giving a small amount or giving a significant amount, continue to increase your faith. When God gifted us with his son Jesus, He gave out of love (John 3:16). Let love motivate us along a path of continuous generosity.

Another heated debate amongst Christians is whether to give

the tithe and offerings off of gross income or net income. I'm going to preface my answer based on my personal testimony, church statistics, and scripture. Let me first tell you my giving origin story. There was a time in my early twenties where I wasn't giving the tithe or offerings at all for about six months. Things were very stressful at work. The stress was heavily weighing on my performance. I truly believed I was going to get fired.

One night while crying out to God during prayer, I broke down, crying in desperation. I said something to the tune of "Lord, I need you to help me! I know that you're Jehovah Jireh, my provider!" Not even a few seconds later, the Holy Spirit spoke to me. He said, "Jason, you call me Jehovah Jireh, but you don't believe me." Ouch. I wept for what felt like an hour. But the Holy Spirit also told me, "But Jason, I'm going to show you that I'm your provider." This was the catalyst for me to start giving again. I started tithing the very next paycheck. I gave off my net pay.

Within five months, I got a new job with more pay, two raises, and money from a small fender bender. The Lord was showing me how faithful He was as my provider. The next big test for me came when I got an unexpected bonus. I was pretty excited about what God was doing, so in the spirit of thanksgiving, I decided to give $500 out of the bonus. This amount was over ten percent. Just when I started to feel pretty good about myself, the Holy Spirit interrupted my train of thought. "No, Jason. I don't want you to give $500. I want you to give $1000." My jaw about hit the floor, and my heart felt like it got stuck in my throat. I had never given any kind of gift that large before!

At church, we had a Valentine's event coming up and help was needed paying for catered food for the event. I responded to the Holy Spirit's challenge and gave the $1000. Later on, I found out that exact amount was needed to help contribute to a nice meal for all the couples at the event. That experience melted my heart, and for the first time in my life, I understood what Jesus meant when he said, "it is more blessed to give than to receive (Acts 20:35)."

The Lord worked on my heart all the way up until getting married in the area of generosity. He had to cleanse me from all the fear and garbage I had in my life concerning money and my family background. That's a story for another day. Today I better understand why the Lord took me down this path. He was molding me for one of His daughters. My wife is the most generous person that I know. She truly gives freely, both of herself and with money. He couldn't have a broken person be the spiritual head of a generous person. God used my wife to help move me further down the journey to a generous heart. I now give off of gross rather than net pay.

According to NonProfit Source, the following trends were captured in the 2019 Church Giving Report: people who tithe only make up around 10-25% of any congregation, on average Christians give 2.5% of their income to churches, and only 1% of $75,000+ earning families give 10% of their income.[20] With those kinds of statistics, I'm not sure why there's so much debate about gross vs. net and what amount to give because 1) most church attendees don't tithe, and 2) most church attendees give a much smaller percentage of their income.

Proverbs 3:9-10 says to "**Honor** the LORD with your wealth and with the **firstfruits** of all your produce; then your barns will be filled with plenty, and your vats will be bursting with wine." I'm not a theologian or scholar on the subject of giving, but I try to look at the principle of the matter. Keep God **first and central** when it comes to giving. Because of who He is and what He's done for me, I've "purposed in my heart" to prioritize Him financially over everything else. Secondly, He's the fire that burns within me to carry a spirit of thanksgiving.

We've already touched on the importance of saving wisely from a business perspective. We will discuss the equal importance of doing so for your personal finances. There are three primary reasons to save money: for emergencies, for large purchases, and for retirement.

According to the 2018 Survey of Household Economics and Decision Making, 40% of Americans struggle to come up with $400 for an unexpected bill.[21] This is astounding! For emergencies, set aside 3-12 months of expenses to create a buffer between you and life. Life being Murphy's Law. Anything that can happen, will happen (flat tire, home repair, 911 hospital visit, emergency flight for a funeral, etc.). If you live in a two-income home with stable jobs, you may consider a three-month emergency fund. If you are self-employed or a one-income family, you might consider a six- or twelve-month emergency fund. If you are approaching retirement, set aside 24-36 months of expenses.

To understand this pre-retirement strategy, think about the faucet in your sink. Notice how you can turn the water pressure up and down based on what you're doing (doing dishes vs. washing hands). The thought here is to have the flexibility to dial down your retirement distributions and instead draw from your emergency fund to slow your withdrawal rate.

Two of the largest purchases you'll make in your lifetime will be a car and a home. Save up and pay cash for a used vehicle because new cars lose up to 40% of their value within five years.[22] Buy a used car, 2-3 years old under 40,000 miles. Get it inspected by a mechanic as part of the terms of purchase. Pay cash for a car so that a monthly car note doesn't eat up your income. According to NerdWallet, as of 2018, the average monthly car loan on a new car is $530, $381 for a used car, and $430 for a lease.[23] Yikes!

Before buying a home, pay off your debts, and build up your emergency fund. Doing so will free up more available dollars for you to save up a large down payment. If you put 20% down on a home, you will avoid PMI (private mortgage insurance). Private mortgage insurance protects the lender against calamity, not you. Why pay for something that's in someone else's favor? Using a $100,000 mortgage as an example, 1% of PMI added to your monthly mort-gage payment would result in you paying an additional $1,000 per year ($83.33/month).[24] Consider taking out a 15- or 20-year fixed-rate conventional mortgage rather than a 30-year to save thousands of dollars in interest due to a shorter term. Make sure your mort-gage payment is around 25% of your monthly take-home pay. This will ensure you don't buy more house than you can afford.

The third and final reason to save money is for retirement. Believe it or not, the Bible encourages investing by touching on some important investing practices. Ecclesiastes 11:2 NLT refer-ences the practice of diversification: "But divide your invest-ments among many places, for you do not know what risks may lie ahead."[25]

Let me make a very important distinction about the world-view of retirement and the scriptural view. The only example of retirement in scripture is that of the Levites in Numbers 8:23-26.

"And the Lord spoke to Moses, saying, 'This applies to the Levites: from twenty-five years old and upward they shall come to do duty in the service of the tent of meeting. And from the age of fifty years they shall withdraw from the duty of the service and serve no more. They minister to their brothers in the tent of meeting by keeping guard, but they shall do no service. Thus shall you do to the Levites in assigning their duties.'"

There is no mention of retirement in scripture the way the world portrays it (vacation, travel, sunset your life, etc.). It is of my personal opinion that we look at the retirement season as a purpose-filled second half of life. We should consider using our gifts to mentor the next generation, pray about Holy Spirit-inspired vocation, and give generously to spread the gospel of Jesus Christ around the world. Will you spend time with family and cross a few things off your bucket list? Sure. But the second half of our lives should focus on seeking direction from the Lord.

You'll want to invest so that you have enough money for expenses in your elderly years. Your youthful years are when you are vibrant, strong, and have more earning potential. This doesn't mean that as you get older, you won't have energy. It also doesn't mean that you can't earn a significant income in your later years. Health is a prominent factor for why you should focus on saving during your younger years. One of the most important considerations leading into your later years is to reduce your expenses and simplify lifestyle. You'll no longer have the same financial obligations (children, education, etc.) from decades before. Seek the counsel of an investment professional to run financial models of what you could potentially end up with in your retirement nest egg. Depending on your age and budget, ask to see what the outcomes of investing 10%, 15%, or 20% of your income over 20-40 years could look like. Inquire about how they get compensated because, sadly, that can drive what an advisor recommends to you, and that may not be in your best interest. Additionally, educate yourself on investing concepts like rate of return, compound interest, diversification, and dollar-cost averaging so you can have a more fruitful discussion with an investment professional. For more information about retirement education and finding a trusted financial advisor, check out these resources:

- https://www.investopedia.com/
- https://www.morningstar.com/
- https://kingdomadvisors.com/
- https://soundmindinvesting.com/
- https://www.eventidefunds.com/
- https://www.ronblue.com/
- https://www.thrivent.com/
- https://www.napfa.org/
- https://www.garrettplanningnetwork.com/
- https://www.xyplanningnetwork.com/

We now have a focused game plan for giving generously and saving wisely. It's time to round out our personal finance journey with what it means to live appropriately. Living appropriately involves building and maintaining solid financial habits. The good news is that we don't have to go far to discover these habits. They are presented to us right in God's Word. The Bible gives us six tenets around the suitable handling of money:

1. God is our provider.
2. Create and follow a budget.
3. Spend less than you earn.
4. Live obligation-free.
5. Don't co-sign.
6. Avoid get rich quick schemes.

Habit #1 - God Is Our Provider: Philippians 4:19 says, "And my God will supply every need of yours according to his riches in glory in Christ Jesus."

It's very easy to get caught up in the benefits of income and status that our occupations bring. But job security doesn't come from man. God, in His love and sovereignty, blessed us with gifts and talents to produce income. It is He who gave us the power to obtain wealth. God gets the glory for our talent, the job that produces the income, and any success associated with our earning potential. Don't fall for the world's seductive temptation that we are "self-made" men and women. We are "God-made" children created in His image. Jehovah Jireh is our provider.

Habit #2 – Create And Follow A Budget: Proverbs 21:5 says, "The plans of the diligent lead surely to abundance, but everyone who is hasty comes only to poverty."

Planning is a character trait of someone who is diligent. We plan for all kinds of events like vacations, kid activities, birthdays, and holidays. What about the component that funds all of these activities? That's what a budget (spending plan) accomplishes. John Maxwell shares with us that "a budget is telling your money where to go, instead of wondering where it went."[26]

When we don't have a budget in place, we deny ourselves the feedback loop that displays the health of our spending progress.

Budgeting takes a little time to get used to in the beginning. After about 90 days of budgeting, however, it'll become muscle memory.

I recommend two pre-budget exercises to get you going in the right direction:

1) Go through your last one or two bank statements. This will visualize "where" the money has been going. Look for patterns like high dollar amounts, frequented retailers, subscriptions, and seasonal transactions.

2) Keep a spending journal for 30 days. Record every single daily transaction. You should derive similar learnings as the above exercise. The difference with this practice is that you begin the discipline of documenting your transactions as they happen.

When creating a budget, make sure you start with what I call the **four essentials**: **food**, **housing** (including rent/mortgage, and utilities), **clothing**, and **transportation**. If you prioritize these, you'll live to fight another day. Continue listing out all other potential expenses, such as insurance. For direction on budget categories and percentage allocations, see Lee Jenkins' graphic "Your Budget Percentage Guidelines."[27]

Helpful Tools

YOUR BUDGET PERCENTAGE GUIDELINES

Category	Percent of Income (after giving and taxes)
Housing	25 – 38%
Food	10 – 15%
Transportation	10 – 15%
Insurance	3 – 7%
Debts	0 – 10%
Entertainment/Recreation	4 – 7%
Clothing	4 – 6%
Savings	5 – 10%
Medical/Dental	4 – 8%
Miscellaneous	4 – 8%
School/Child care	5 – 10%
Investments	0 – 15%

As you complete your budget, you'll be creating what's known as a Zero-Based Budget. It's just a fancy term for assigning every single dollar of income a responsibility for the month. One trick of the trade that my wife and I do with our budget is create a line item called **"Buffer."** This is a pre-determined amount of money that will remain untouched during the month. As you transition into the next month, this untouched money becomes a line item under your income section known as **"Rollover."** If you incorporate this tactic month over month, you'll stop living paycheck to paycheck.

For tracking purposes, it's very important to use a budgeting tool or software. Generally speaking, there are four kinds of budgeting platforms: **pen and paper**, **spreadsheet-based** (Ex. Excel, Google Sheets), **computer software** (Ex. Quicken, Banktivity), and **mobile/web-based** (Ex. EveryDollar, YNAB - You Need A Budget, Mint, Goodbudget, MoneyPatrol, Mvelopes). One is not necessarily better than the other. Pick the one that best meets your needs (i.e., ease of use, user interface, cost, etc.).

Done the with love and respect, developing a budget with your spouse will enhance intimacy and communication. Intimacy and communication can build in (but not limited to) four ways while discussing money: physical closeness, transparency, sacrifice, and commitment.

Physical Closeness - There's something about sitting in close proximity and discussing a vulnerable topic like money that can help bring people closer together.

Transparency - Expressing your financial dreams, fears, and goals together will build empathy and keep you on the same page. Don't hide anything from your spouse.

Sacrifice - Each of you have certain wants or preferences that differ from the other. And that's okay. Mutually put aside your pride and selfishness to sacrifice for each other. I recommend that both spouses have a fun money section in the budget where they can spend as they please (within reason, of course).

Commitment – You've talked the talk. Now you must walk the walk. If something comes up during the month and you need to change a line item on the budget, talk about it with your spouse. Mutually submit to one another by carrying out the spending plan as agreed and or revised.

Habit #3 – Spend Less Than You Earn: Luke 16:1-2 NASB: "Now He was also saying to the disciples, 'There was a rich man who had a manager, and this *manager* was reported to him as **squandering his possessions**. And he called him and said to him, 'What is this I hear about you? **Give an accounting of your management**, for you can no longer be manager.'"[28]

To ensure we have enough to provide for our household, we must spend less than we earn. When we overspend recklessly, it's a form of "squandering" God's resources. Understanding why you're purchasing something is of paramount importance. Before you buy a product or service, ask yourself, "Is this a want or a need?" If shopping functions as a kind of therapy for you, you'd do well to try to identify the source of discontentment.

The Bible warns us in particular about one source of discontentment: the love of money.

Love of Money

Hebrews 13:5:

"Keep your life free from **love of money**, and be *content* with what you have, for he has said, "I will never leave you nor forsake you.""

Have you ever heard someone say, "money is the root of all evil?" That is actually a false statement and a misquoting of scripture. That phrase is written in the "Book of Nowhere." The "love of money" is the root of all evil (1 Timothy 6:10). When one makes a pursuit of wealth the endgame, they slip into a trap, by way of irrational and destructive ambition, which causes a freefall into ruin.

God ultimately desires us to be content. Pastor Kunle Akindoju of King's Court Chapel has a wonderful definition of contentment: "wanting what you already have rather than having what you want."[29] The good news is that contentment can be learned. The Apostle Paul points this out to us in Philippians 4:11: "Not that I am speaking of being in need, for I have learned in whatever situation I am to be content." I believe that Paul learned the "great gain in godliness with contentment (1 Timothy 6:6)" by resting on the words of Jesus in Matthew 6:31-34.

"Therefore do not be anxious, saying, 'What shall we eat?' or 'What shall we drink?' or 'What shall we wear?' For the Gentiles seek after all these things, and your heavenly Father knows that you need them all. But seek first the kingdom of God and his righteousness, and all these things will be added to you. Therefore do not be anxious about tomorrow, for tomorrow will be anxious for itself. Sufficient for the day is its own trouble."

Habit #4 – Live Obligation Free: Romans 13:7-8 – "**Pay to all what is owed to them**: taxes to whom taxes are owed, revenue to whom revenue is owed, respect to whom respect is owed, honor to whom honor is owed. **Owe no one anything**, except to love each other, for the one who loves another has fulfilled the law."

God wants us to live a life devoted to Him, not obligated to the distracting things of this world. Being free of constraints keeps us in perfect peace because of trust in Him (Isaiah 26:3-4). Avoid debt and pay it off quickly if you have any. Pay your taxes. Tax reduction is fine, wise even. Tax evasion is an integrity violation. Pay employees, distributions, court orders, and revenue of any kind. Give respect and honor when it's deserved.

Habit #5 – Don't Co-Sign: Proverbs 17:18 – "One who lacks sense gives a pledge and puts up security in the presence of his neighbor."

The Bible makes it very clear that being the guarantor for someone else's debt is not wise. Co-signing is only even possible when someone is not creditworthy. The idea is that someone co-signs on a loan with another person to take advantage of their established credit history. Big red flag! Where there's smoke, there's fire when creditworthiness isn't the best. Stats prove this point even more why co-signing is foolish. In a survey by Credit-Cards.com, it was discovered that "38 percent of co-signers had to pay some or all of the loan or credit card bill because the primary borrower did not."[30] Sheesh! Whatever you do, don't co-sign.

Habit #6 – Avoid Get Rich Quick Schemes: Proverbs 13:11 NLT "Wealth from get-rich-quick schemes quickly disappears; wealth from hard work grows over time."[31]

Some people will do anything to make a quick buck. When something sounds too good to be true, it usually is. Wealth builds from hard work over time (Proverbs 21:5). Pray and ask God if it's his will that you apply for a certain job or start a new business venture.

If you will give generously, save wisely, and live appropriately the way God intends, you will be blessed by your faithfulness and obedience. God wants the best for you. He will always do his part; we just have to do ours. Manage well.

For a deeper dive into personal finance, here is a list of great resources:

Books

How To Manage Your Money by Larry Burkett
Debt Free Living by Larry Burkett
Master Your Money by Ron Blue
Never Enough?: 3 Keys To Financial Contentment by Ron Blue
Splitting Heirs by Ron Blue
Your Money Counts by Howard Dayton
Money and Marriage God's Way by Howard Dayton
Free And Clear by Howard Dayton
The Total Money Makeover by Dave Ramsey
Smart Money Smart Kids by Dave Ramsey & Rachel Cruze
Your Life Well Spent by Russ Crosson
Your Money Made Simple by Russ Crosson
The Truth About Money Lies by Russ Crosson

Lee Jenkins On Money by Lee Jenkins
Taking Care of Business by Lee Jenkins
Never Chase A Paycheck Again by Dr. Robert J. Watkins
Money, Possessions, And Eternity by Randy Alcorn
The Seven Money Types by Tommy Brown
7 Money Rules For Life by Mary Hunt
Debt Proof Living by Mary Hunt
Your New Money Mindset by Brad Hewitt
He Spends She Spends by John H. Putnam
God And Money by John Cortines & Gregory Baumer
True Riches by John Cortines & Gregory Baumer
The Sound Mind Investing Handbook by Austin Pryor w/Mark Biller
The Money Challenge by Art Rainer
Love Your Life Not Theirs by Rachel Cruze
Navigating The Mortgage Maze by Dale Vermillion

Websites
https://www.crown.org/
https://compass1.org/
https://www.daveramsey.com/
https://www.jerichoforce.com

CHAPTER TAKEAWAYS

1. God is the owner, and we are His managers (stewards).
2. Three values of a good steward are leadership, wisdom, and discipline.
3. We are called to be active "Marketplace Ambassadors" for Christ, not passive "Monday Morning Atheists."
4. Business and personal finances should both be managed with excellence.

EFFECTIVE LEADERSHIP

"FOR EVEN THE SON OF MAN CAME NOT TO BE SERVED BUT TO SERVE, AND TO GIVE HIS LIFE AS A RANSOM FOR MANY."

— MARK 10:45

"BEING IN POWER IS LIKE BEING A LADY. IF YOU HAVE TO REMIND PEOPLE THAT YOU ARE, YOU AREN'T."

— MARGARET THATCHER

LEAD BY SERVING

One of the most impactful stories I've heard about leadership came from best-selling author and Ramsey Personality Chris Hogan. Before Chris teamed up with Dave Ramsey, he used to work in the financial services industry as a banker. He told of a time where he was newly promoted to a management position and how power-hungry he was. While talking to one of his direct reports, he reminded them of his title. The employee then responded, "Yes, Chris, I know you're in charge because of your title. But show me with your actions that you're in charge."[32] That one statement was forever a gamechanger for him. That story stuck out to me after hearing him speak about it at a conference. When it comes to leadership, people are always watching your actions. The most powerful action and posture you can display is servanthood. There are many kinds of documented leadership styles (transformational, situational, laissez-faire, etc.), but the foundation of them all is servant leadership.

SERVANT LEADERSHIP

The actual term "servant leadership" was coined by Robert K. Greenleaf in his 1970 essay *The Servant As Leader*.[33] Servant leadership was first introduced in principle by Jesus Christ (see Mark 10:45). I believe Jesus Christ was the greatest example we had for modeling servant leadership. He was fully God and fully man. According to critically acclaimed author Ken Blanchard, servant leadership has two parts: setting vision and goals (leadership) and being others first oriented (servant).[34]

Jesus had a very clear vision, which He derived from His heavenly father. John 3:16-17 says, "For God so loved the world, that he gave his only Son, that whoever believes in him should not perish but have eternal life. For God did not send his Son into the world to condemn the world, but in order that the world might be saved through him." Jesus was always about His Father's business, which was kingdom business. In order to execute the Father's vision, Jesus knew He needed to work through people. Disciples were ones whom Jesus called to carry out the vision. For His disciples, He had one main overarching goal for them: to make them fishers of men (spread the gospel). Jesus makes this declaration in Matthew 4:19. And he said to them, "Follow me, and I will make you fishers of men."

Jesus knew the significance of people and their value. He led from a foundation of love and with the attitude of a servant's heart. An extremely powerful example of Christ's sacrificial servanthood was when He washed the disciples' feet.

John 13:5 says, "Then he poured water into a basin and began to wash the disciples' feet and to wipe them with the towel that was wrapped around him."

John 13:14-15 says, "If I then, your Lord and Teacher, have washed your feet, you also ought to wash one another's feet. For I have given you an example, that you also should do just as I have done for you."

Jesus Christ served others because He was hyper-focused on proclaiming good news to the poor, prisoners, the blind, and the oppressed. Jesus Christ was a servant leader incarnate.

CAST VISION

The most effective leaders set a vision for people. Vision answers the outstanding question of "why." Prominent author and speaker Simon Sinek highlights the significance of why using his "Golden Circle" illustration.[35]

The Golden Circle
WHY – Purpose, Belief
HOW – Process, Value Proposition
WHAT – Product, Service

Sinek uses the model to discuss how organizations differentiate themselves from the competition. Most companies market with an "outside in" approach, promoting what and how. Sinek implores that the inverse, an "inside out" approach is more effective. Sinek says, "People don't buy what you do, they buy why you do it."[36]

The Bible gives further insight on vision casting in the book of Habakkuk. Habakkuk 2:2-3 says, "And the Lord answered me: "Write the vision; make it plain on tablets, so he may run who reads it. For still, the vision awaits its appointed time; it hastens to the end—it will not lie. If it seems slow, wait for it; it will surely come; it will not delay." This passage is rich with five key themes.

1. **Write the vision down to make it known.**
2. **Post the vision where people can see it.**
3. **People act when they know and see the vision (target).**
4. **Executing the vision takes time.**
5. **Fulfilling the vision requires patience.**

The Bible artfully discusses the power of what it looks like to have a vision. The Bible also talks about the travesty that comes with a lack of vision. Proverbs 29:18 AMP says, "Where there is no vision [no revelation of God and his word], the people are unrestrained;"[37] **People lose focus and control when there isn't a vision to guide them.** Let's not miss the most important aspect of vision.

Vision comes from God, revealing himself to us, not from business manuals and checklists. There is a unique discovery process and providence that comes with setting a vision. God is always trying to show us something, but we must be open to and aware of what He's doing.

FOLLOWERSHIP

In order to lead effectively, one must first learn how to follow. Lots of emphasis gets put on leadership. And rightfully so. John Maxwell says, "everything rises and falls on leadership."[38] But if we're not careful, we can overlook other important development journeys like "followership." Dictionary.com defines "followership" as "the ability or willingness to follow a leader."[39] There are two words that jump off the page in this definition: ability and willingness. Based on my experience, I believe that one's ability to follow is based on positioning and submission. Positioning in this case, meaning physical proximity and inward intentions, not rank. Good followers have a desire to stay close to the leader because they wholeheartedly believe in the cause. Willingness is a factor of submission. A good follower is willing to yield or cast their vote of being influenced. They are also willing to do the supportive activities or duties necessary to carry out the leader's vision. A great example from scripture of someone who was a great follower before they became a leader was David.

David, Son of Jesse, was anointed to be King of Israel at a young age. He would not, however, become King of Israel until several years later at the age of 30 (2 Samuel 5:4). David was "positioned" to serve King Saul because of his stellar reputation (1 Samuel 16:18). He went on to become Saul's armor-bearer and calmed his anxiety by playing the lyre (1 Samuel 16:21-23). David also demonstrated humble "submission" to the office of king by sparing Saul's life upon having the opportunity to kill him at the Cave of Adullam (1 Samuel 24:10-11). Rather than take the throne for himself by force, David chose to wait on God's timing to take the crown. Position and submission make a good recipe for followership. One parting note on followership, isn't it interesting that the first ask Jesus made of His disciples was a command to "follow Him?"

LEAD WITH HUMILITY

Just like having the heart of a servant, another essential quality for effective leadership is humility. The best definition of humility I've ever heard comes from Pastor and author Rick Warren. Here's an excerpt from his book *The Purpose Driven Life*: "Humility is not thinking less of yourself; it's thinking of yourself less."[40] That is a mouthful of goodness. Humility, as Warren emphasizes, is not a lack of confidence. Leadership requires one to be confident and bold when the time calls. Warren's point about "thinking of yourself less" features a focus on "we" not "me." Good leaders get things done through others. You cannot properly influence others if you're only concerned with yourself. There are three skills that demonstrate a mastery of humility: delegation, multiplication, and vulnerability.

DELEGATION

Did you know people faced business problems in scripture like the need to delegate? Moses, who was called "the deliverer," led the entire nation of Israel out of slavery from Egypt. To be responsible for the well-being of a whole country was probably a huge burden. Perhaps even more than Moses may have been willing to admit. The good news was that Moses wasn't alone. God was with him every step of the way. God used Jethro, Moses' father in law, to bring attention to how cumbersome Moses' day to day workload had become. Jethro sat his son in law down and shared with him some nuggets of wisdom.

Exodus 18:17-23 says, "Moses' father in law said to him, "What you are doing is not good. You and the people with you will certainly wear yourselves out, for the thing is too heavy for you. You are not able to do it alone. Now obey my voice; I will give you advice, and God be with you! You shall represent the people before God and bring their cases to God, and you shall warn them about the statutes and laws and make them know how they must walk and what they must do.

Moreover, look for able men from all the people, men who fear God, who are trustworthy and hate a bribe, and place such men over the people as chiefs of thousands, of hundreds, of fifties, and of tens. And let them judge the people at all times. Every great matter they shall bring to you, but any small matter they shall decide themselves. So, it will be easier for you, and they will bear the burden with you. If you do this, God will direct you, you will be able to endure, and all these people also will go to their place in peace."

There is golden advice in these few verses given by Jethro. Let's unpack some of the themes for learning how to delegate.

1. **Understand the brutal reality of what you're doing now (v.17).**
2. **Continuing alone will lead to burnout (v.18).**
3. **Get clear on what YOU NEED to do (v.19-20).**
4. **Find talented, faithful, trustworthy people to help you (v.21).**
5. **Delegate out the simple tasks (v.22).**
6. **Take on only the complex tasks (v.22).**

An inability to delegate is rooted in two debilitating qualities: pride and fear. Every sin and misstep derive from these two because of the fall of man back in the Garden of Eden. Pride began in Lucifer's (who became Satan) heart before he was ousted from Heaven (Luke 10:18). Satan then used curiosity and cleverness to tempt Adam and Eve by promoting the thought of being like God (what Satan wanted all along). Fear suddenly came upon Adam and Eve when God questioned them about what they had done. Adam blamed Eve and Eve blamed the serpent. Men and women, to this day, struggle with taking responsibility for their actions as a result.

Pride is all about me and the lack of we. In business, there arises this propensity to believe that one really can do it all. No different from believing one could be like God (not need God). Bottom line, pride demonstrates a lack of trust in God. Pride moves us away from relationships rather than towards them, resulting in isolation. Author Stephen Mansfield lists Choosing Isolation as Warning Sign #2 for a sign of a leadership crash. He goes on to say, "When you isolate yourself, you're continually cutting yourself off from feedback from those who know and love you."[41] Thank God Moses had Jethro!

Fear paralyzes us from taking action. Because the nature of business is cyclical, it's not unusual for business owners or employees to try their hardest to control outcomes. This also demonstrates a lack of trust in God. Only God knows the begin-

ning from the end. It's our responsibility to take steps of faith
and trust God to do the rest.

Now that we understand the impact of not delegating, let's
talk about some of the potential benefits of delegation. We can
learn from Moses' response to his father in law on the subject.

Exodus 18:23-24 "If you do this, God will direct you, you will
be able to endure, and all these people also will go to their place
in peace. So, Moses listened to the voice of his father-in-law and
did all that he had said."

Verse 23 gives us three fruits of delegation:

1. **Direction (from God)**
2. **Endurance (sustainability)**
3. **Peace**

Do not skip over the importance of verse 24. Listen. The
benefits of delegation are conditional. One must make the "con-
scious decision" and "willing act" to delegate. Delegation is a
matter of wisdom for effective leadership.

MULTIPLICATION

Liz Wiseman's book *Multipliers* classifies people into two
distinct categories: Diminishers and Multipliers.[42] Each has a
different plan in the workplace. Wiseman studied both groups of
people and developed a model to distinguish their characteristics.

The Five Disciplines Of The Multiplier

1. **The Diminisher is an Empire Builder. The
   Multiplier is a Talent Magnet.**
2. **The Diminisher is a Tyrant. The Multiplier is a
   Liberator.**
3. **The Diminisher is a Know-It-All. The
   Multiplier is a Challenger.**

4. **The Diminisher is a Decision Maker. The Multiplier is a Debate Maker.**
5. **The Diminisher is a Micromanager. The Multiplier is an Investor.**

Using Wiseman's model, let's look at examples of a Diminisher and a Multiplier in scripture.

Diminisher – Haman

1. Hoards resources and underutilizes talent – Esther 3:10-11
2. Creates a tense environment that suppresses people's thinking and capability – Esther 3:5-6, Esther 4:3
3. Gives directives that showcases how much they know – Esther 3:8-9
4. Makes centralized, abrupt decisions that confuse the organization – Esther 3:13-15
5. Drives results through their personal involvement – Esther 5:12-14

Multiplier – Abraham

1. Attracts talented people and uses them at their highest point of contribution – Genesis 14:13-16
2. Creates an intense environment that requires people's best thinking and work – Genesis 24
3. Defines an opportunity that causes people to stretch – Genesis 20
4. Drives sound decisions through rigorous debate – Genesis 18:22-26
5. Gives other people the ownership for results and invests in their success – Genesis 13:8-9

People, generally speaking, don't set out to be diminishers.

Misplaced thoughts, feelings, and decisions result in people making poor choices. These choices have a recurring theme: self-ishness. Choose today what kind of leader you want to be. A Multiplying Abraham who views people as "resourceful" or a Diminishing Haman who views people as resources? Choose.

VULNERABILITY

Throughout my life, I've learned that transparency begets more transparency. Not just on a personal level, but on a professional level. I have seen powerful relationships get forged in the work-place—long-lasting, fruitful friendships and partnerships. Edgar and Peter Schein explain this relational phenomenon as part of a continuum called the Four Levels of Relationships. Let's investi-gate each stage.

Four Levels of Relationships[43]

Level Minus 1: Total impersonal domination

Level 1: Transactional role and rule-based supervision, service, and most forms of "professional" helping relationships

Level 2: Personal cooperative, trusting relationships as in friendships and effective teams

Level 3: Emotionally intimate total mutual commitments

The Schein Father-Son duo go on to explain that the critical differentiator of the levels is what's known as "personization." According to the Scheins, personization is "the process of mutu-ally building a working relationship with a fellow employee, teammate, boss, subordinate, or colleague based on trying to see that person as a whole, not just in the role that he or she may occupy at the moment."[44] Every relationship requires an invest-ment of sorts. This model, dare I say, is fueled by transparency and vulnerability. They are the wind beneath the sails of the personization process.

Founder of Chick-Fil-A, Truett Cathy, knew that customer service was the lifeblood of business. He was ever focused on how he could deliver more customer value and satisfaction. One simple ask Cathy made of all his restaurants was that when a customer says, "thank you," his employees were to respond purposefully with the words "my pleasure." Legend has it that Cathy was enamored with a Ritz-Carlton employee who responded "my pleasure" when he said thank you one time during a hotel stay. Amazing how just a couple of words can ignite a fire of impact! The extra mile Chick-Fil-A goes draws customers into a deeper, more meaningful interaction. Chick-Fil-A took what is considered a highly transactional industry (fast food retail) and flipped it on its head. They intentionally sought out Level 2 and Level 3 relationships with anyone who came through their restaurant doors. It has been said that Truett Cathy once went on record saying, "We aren't really in the chicken business, we are in the people business."[45]

How to build relationships with others is a motif that recurs throughout the Bible. Christianity is about having a personal relationship with Jesus Christ. Because He first loved us, His love created the capacity and desire for us to love and build relationships with others. This then allows us to go and make disciples as Jesus has commanded. A major part of how one shares the gospel and makes disciples is through being vulnerable. Vulnerable in speech, thought, and action. Let's delve into Biblical vulnerability.

Vulnerable In Speech – 2 Corinthians 6:11-13 AMP[46]

"We are speaking freely to you, Corinthians [we are keeping nothing back], and our heart is opened wide. There is no limit to our affection for you, but you are limited in your own affection [for us]. Now in the same way as a fair exchange [for our love toward you]—I am speaking as [I would] to children—open wide [your hearts] *to us* also."

Vulnerable In Thought – Philippians 2:3-5 NLT[47]

"Don't be selfish; don't try to impress others. Be humble, thinking of others as better than yourselves. Don't look out only for your own interests, but take an interest in others, too. You must have the same attitude Christ Jesus had."

Vulnerable In Action – Matthew 22:39 (Partial)

"You shall love your neighbor as yourself."

We are living in difficult times that are growing more divisive by the day. Our places of work are being infected with artificial and superficial attitudes. People desire to be led but aren't sure if they can bring their "entire self" to work. Be a leader that unlocks the best in others by tearing down the walls of a phony work culture.

CHAPTER TAKEAWAYS

1. People lose focus and control when there isn't a vision to guide them.
2. An inability to delegate is rooted in two debilitating qualities: pride and fear.
3. Misplaced thoughts, feelings, and decisions result in people making poor choices.

VALUES ARE GOLDEN

"KEEP YOUR HEART WITH ALL VIGILANCE, FOR FROM IT FLOW THE SPRINGS OF LIFE."

— PROVERBS 4:23

"YOUR ACTIONS SPEAK SO LOUDLY THAT I CANNOT HEAR WHAT YOU SAY."

— RALPH WALDO EMERSON

VALUES ACT AS A BAROMETER

A barometer is "any instrument that measures atmospheric pressure; anything that indicates changes."[48] There are all kinds of pressures in business from quotas, profit margins, and market trends, to executive board expectations. These daily pressures and conditions reveal who we really are. Will we rise to the occasion? Or will we crumble when the going gets tough? An unspoken measure of our integrity comes down to values. Values act as a barometer for our character.

When we think that nobody is watching, God is. He is the ultimate judge of our character. 1 Samuel 16:7 (partial) says, "... For the Lord sees not as man sees: man looks on the outward appearance, but the Lord looks on the heart." We can certainly fool others. We can even fool ourselves at times. We cannot fool God. We must conduct business through the lens of righteousness, not the world system.

INTENT IS FELT RATHER THAN MEASURED

A person's character is like an onion. There are many layers to it. Focus on the "layers," not the stench of the metaphor. Our backgrounds and experiences help determine where we are, but ultimately our intent guides what we do. Intent is a tricky thing because it cannot be measured; it's simply felt by others. God is the only person who can measure the heart. If we can back up for just a moment to bring leadership (influence) in the equation, it will help us unpack intent.

In Mack Story's book *Defining Influence*, he builds out the foundational layers of leadership, which he defines as influence. Story further says that "the foundation of influence is trust."[49] Stephen M. R. Covey reiterates the power of trust with his saying: "Everything moves at the speed of trust."[50] But the foundation of trust is intent. Values, or the lack of them, establish a person's intent. Story posits that intent comes down to what kind of person you are. If you want to become a better leader, become a better person. If you want your intent to be positively felt by others, you must become better. This point couldn't be summed up better than by actor Stephen Amell who played Oliver Queen (AKA the Green Arrow) on The CW's *Arrow*: "To do this, I must become someone else. I must become something else."[51]

As marketplace ambassadors, we must be acutely self-aware. Aware that our nature, without the guidance of the Holy Spirit, is inherently hypocritical. Jeremiah 17:9-10 says, "The heart is deceitful above all things, and desperately sick; who can understand it? I the Lord search the heart and test the mind, to give every man according to his ways, according to the fruit of his deeds." We must take up our cross daily (Matthew 16:24-26) so that we can serve both customer and employee needs for the glory of God. Taking up our cross means dying to self (spirit focus over flesh focus) as well as going to God to deal with our sinful issues. Sin masks our intent. Intent should be a radiant light to shine, rather than a deceitful shadow to cast on others.

PRESSURE REVEALS WHO WE ARE

Diamonds are comprised of just one element, which is carbon, and yet are considered to be the hardest substance on planet Earth. Diamonds undergo tremendous pressure and are usually buried deep within the Earth. They emerge on the Earth's surface within volcanos.[52] Amazingly, heat and depth produce one of nature's most beautiful creations. I can't help but draw our attention to the words *heat* and *depth*. Similar to diamonds, humans undergo adverse conditions. The intense pressure and treacherous depth of trials tend to whittle away any false pretense. The big question is, what's left when you come to the end of yourself?

I would ask you to consider what kind of values you have when the going gets tough? Business is hard. Go ahead and say that out loud. Work gets stressful. I have excellent news for you, though. Jesus cares about you during the workday! He wants the best for you. But He also expects us to be men and women of integrity. Jesus is a keeper of his word, and He asked that we do the same in Matthew 5:37 NLT "Just say a simple, 'Yes, I will,' or 'No, I won't.' Anything beyond this is from the evil one."[53] Cast your cares upon Jesus (1 Peter 5:7) and let Him change your heart. The world's standards fall when tension rises. Don't be like the rest of the world and conform, rather transform (Romans 12:2) and be a values-driven person.

One key value to incorporate into your life and work is joy. It seems strange to mention joy in the midst of daily pressures, but that's what is available to us (from God) if we choose it. James 1:2 actually tells us to "count it all joy" when we experience trials. Joy is crucial to experiencing peace because it is how we derive strength from God (Nehemiah 8:10). Strength to do what? Make high character decisions when the heat is turned up the most. Stay honest when everyone else wants to be shady. Be steadfast when others want to give in.

VALUES SHAPE BEHAVIOR

James 2:18 says, "But someone will say, "You have faith, and I have works." Show me your faith apart from your works, and I will show you my faith by my works." Values and behaviors have kindred parallels. Some will say, "You have a precious value system or moral compass. I don't need that. I just act according to the situation." In the same vein as James, I would argue to "Show me your behavior apart from your values, and I will show you my behavior by my values." Our values shape our human behavior.

PRINCIPLES

Values help shape behavior in the form of principles. If princi-ples were a body part, they would be the "heart" of values. The difference between values and principles is the rate of change. For example, a CEO might change or add to a company's core values over time based on any number of reasons specific to the situation (key learnings, shifts in company culture, etc.). Princi-ples, on the other hand, are rooted in rules and guidelines that influence your actions. Let's take a look at two examples of value-principle pairs.

Value: Frugality
Principle: We don't buy anything unless we can afford it. Period.

Value: Integrity
Principle: We don't lie under any circumstance. Regardless of the audience, situation, or job title. Period.

We see here in the above examples that the value holds a parent relationship to the child principle. The principle acts in the spirit of the foundational value. A strong foundation is critical to the success of any organization.

Jesus Christ agreed that things should be built on a good foundation. He tells the story of the wise and foolish builders to illustrate the importance.

Matthew 7:24-27 "Everyone then who hears these words of mine and does them will be like a wise man who built his house on the rock. And the rain fell, and the floods came, and the winds blew and beat on that house, but it did not fall, because it had been founded on the rock. And everyone who hears these words of mine and does not do them will be like a foolish man who built his house on the sand. And the rain fell, and the floods came, and the winds blew and beat against that house, and it fell, and great was the fall of it."

Take a look at some of the themes from Jesus' story:

1. **Listen and act on what you hear.**
2. **A solid foundation is wise.**
3. **Solid foundations endure storms.**
4. **Listening without action has consequences.**
5. **A weak foundation is foolish.**
6. **Weak foundations fall with great magnitude.**

As business owners and employees, we are the builders in this story. Jesus Christ is the solid rock. The sand is the world's system. Any foundation not built on Christ will fail. He must be the focal point of why and how we live out our faith. The same is true of our values. Our values need to reflect the image of Jesus. A clarifying and terrifying question to ask yourself: Do my personal and organizational values demonstrate Christ to others?

ETHICS

Ethics are the "brain trust" of values. Dictionary.com defines ethics as "a system of moral principles."[54] Ethics are basically moral principles with shoes on. But what does it mean to be moral? To whom does mankind answer to? If you've accepted Jesus Christ as your Lord and Savior, then He is your master. Those who have not rely on themselves or another entity. Accepting Christ makes us partakers of the divine nature of God. When your nature changes, your morals change. 2 Peter 1:3-4 tells us that the byproduct of partaking in the divine nature of Christ causes us to "escape the corruption that is in the world because of sinful desire." Think about the level of bribery and extortion that occurs in business dealings. Consider the influence it has on society. Jesus calls us into a godly way of buying, selling, and negotiating to shine His light on the darkness.

When salvation takes place, one is saved "for good works (Ephesians 2:10)." The good versus evil dichotomy is expressed throughout scripture. The first moral demonstration man had from God was the ten commandments given to Moses. Known as "the law," the commandments set a standard for righteous living and symbolized man's need for a savior. Any work outside of the will of God is compromised living. Work is a "good work" that God commissioned back in the Garden of Eden. He seeks to teach us to own our reliance on Him in everything we do (Proverbs 3:5-6). Business is no different. God is good all the time. All the time, God is good. We learn good from Him. This leaves us with knowledge of what surely is good versus what surely is sinful. Let's inspect what the Bible says about expectations around good and evil.

James 4:17: "So whoever knows the right thing to do and fails to do it, for him it is sin."
Proverbs 11:3: "The integrity of the upright guides them, but the crookedness of the treacherous destroys them."
Psalms 34:14: "Turn away from evil and do good; seek peace and pursue it."

Still think values are all touchy feely? Don't believe values affect the direction of companies? Read this powerful excerpt from Dina Dwyer-Owens' *Values, Inc.: How Incorporating Values Into Business And Life Change The World*

COMPANIES THAT CHANGE THE PARADIGM

On Valentine's Day 2007, a JetBlue flight bound for Cancun, Mexico, was trapped on the tarmac for more than ten hours. The passengers were locked in a plane with no power, no food, inadequate lavatories, and no explanation for the delay. What made the whole ordeal even more infuriating was that the entire time, the terminal was in sight.
When the media picked up the news about the stranded passengers, the public response was a furor. Unlike many companies that would have put their public relations team into frenetic overdrive, JetBlue did not rationalize or excuse its behavior. Instead, the company openly admitted its mistake and apologized for the inexcusable delay.
But the people at JetBlue didn't stop there. They immediately got to work on creating a "Customer Bill of Rights" to ensure the company held itself accountable for any future delays or unforeseeable inconveniences by giving customers vouchers for future travel.[55]

Values are golden.

CHAPTER TAKEAWAYS

1. Values act as a barometer for our character.
2. Principles are the "heart" of values.
3. Ethics are the "brain trust" of values.

FAIL TO PLAN, PLAN TO FAIL

"COMMIT YOUR WORK TO THE LORD, AND YOUR PLANS WILL BE ESTABLISHED."

— PROVERBS 16:3

"UNLESS COMMITMENT IS MADE, THERE ARE ONLY PROMISES AND HOPES, BUT NO PLANS."

— PETER F. DRUCKER

PLANNING IS WISDOM

Plans may or may not succeed in business. But the principle of "planning" is very important. Planning is simply a matter of wisdom. And wisdom is the proper application of knowledge. Have you ever been in a meeting for a new initiative? Think about a time where you forgot a really important detail. How did it make you feel? What was the result of leaving out the important piece of information? Those situations usually don't end well or get the expected outcome. The Bible lays out to us what's at stake when we don't take time out to plan. Proverbs 21:5 says,

"The plans of the diligent lead surely to abundance, but everyone who is hasty comes only to poverty."

There are some core remarks nested within this proverb. Notice the effect of the "plans of the diligent." They "surely lead to abundance." Dictionary.com defines diligence as "constant and earnest effort to accomplish what is undertaken; persistent exertion of body or mind."[56] Diligence is a commended quality referenced throughout scripture. The word "abundance" in this passage is also significant. Abundance (or advantage) is translated here in Hebrew as "mowthar," meaning "pre-eminence, abundance, profit, and superiority."[57] On the other hand, "everyone who is hasty comes only to poverty." Rushing isn't just physically wasteful. It can be spiritually, mentally, and emotionally as well. Without the leading of the Holy Spirit, haste advances a cause that lacks clarity, focus, and insight. Planning, coupled with diligence, puts the wisdom of God in action for your benefit.

DEEDING YOUR WORK

Turning over our work and business to God is a lot like signing a house deed. A deed is a legal document between buyer and seller that transfers the ownership rights of a property. We learned back in chapter 2 that we are stewards. God is the owner, and we are managers. From a planning standpoint, acknowledging a transfer of ownership to God demonstrates faith in Him, dependency on Him, and humility. Proverbs 9:10 says, "The fear of the Lord is the beginning of wisdom, and knowledge of the Holy One is insight." When you deed your work to God, you demonstrate wisdom by reverencing him and intentionally learning about his nature. No plan will execute without Jesus Christ because he is "the foundation (1 Corinthians 3:11)" and "the cornerstone (Ephesians 2:20-21)" of all things.

Best-selling Biblical Finance teacher Howard Dayton takes participants through a transformational deeding exercise in his Compass small group studies. Though this is done through the lens of personal finance, I strongly consider doing this exercise if you're a business owner. This will help remind you of and symbolize who the business really belongs to. The format looks like the following:[58]

This Deed, Made The
_____ Day Of _____, 20_____

From:
To: The Lord

I (We) Transfer To The Lord The Ownership Of The Following Possessions:

Witnesses who will help hold us accountable to recognize the Lord's ownership:

_____

_____

Signed by the stewards of the possessions above:

_____

_____

INCOMPREHENSIBLE COUNSEL

Three of the best people you can have in your life to consult you on future plans (employer or employee) are a good coach, mentor, and teacher. Coaches help unlock the potential that's already within someone. Mentors are seasoned individuals who provide advice and guidance. Teachers expose new concepts and break down the complex into simple, learnable pieces. People associated with these three roles are able to do this because of their ample life experience and ability to give wise counsel.

Ron Blue, founder of Ronald Blue Trust (wealth management and trust services), is a living example of what wise counsel can lead to. In his book, *Never Enough?: 3 Keys to Financial Contentment*, he tells the story of a man named John, who asked him if it was okay to continue living in the expensive dream home he and his wife bought.[59] Ron Blue responded, "John, I am not the one to answer that question for you. Have you asked God that question? What would God have you to do?" John labored in prayer several weeks, and the Lord instructed him to use the new home as a place of ministry in the city they lived in. He and his wife went on to hold outreach events, dinners, and all kinds of impactful community meetings in that house. What a difference wise counsel can make on preparation.

While men and women can give excellent, timely advice, the greatest counsel any of us can receive comes directly from God. Several hundred years before Jesus' birth in Bethlehem, the prophet Isaiah prophesied about the character of Jesus. His account was recorded in Isaiah 9:6 "For to us a child is born, to us a son is given; and the government shall be upon his shoulder, and his name shall be called **Wonderful Counselor**, Mighty God, Everlasting Father, Prince of Peace." We normally see this passage read during the Christmas season, but there's more to uncover here. Jesus isn't just referred to as "Counselor" but "Wonderful Counselor." The level of counsel that He provides is incomprehensible or limitless. Not only is there no limit to His counsel, but also Jesus holds full mastery over the domain of business. Jesus was basically a walking MBA with unlimited business acumen. I don't know about you, but I'm not launching any product, service, project, or initiative without consulting the King of Kings.

SKILLFUL LIVING

Some people view life in black or white. But this broken and fractured world exists more in the grey area. Business certainly involves a lot of grey because there's so much to handle. People, process, technology, etc. It can be stressful and overwhelming at times. What if I told you that God gave us a "superpower" to help execute our work and run our businesses? That superpower is the wisdom of God. Let's look at how wisdom is chronicled in the Bible.

King Solomon was the wisest man who ever walked the Earth. His wisdom far surpassed what normal human insight can discern (1 Kings 4:29-34). He loved the Lord, walked upright, and recognized his inexperience to govern God's people justly. Solomon was given wisdom because he "asked" God for it (1 Kings 3:1-15). God blessed him with "a wise and discerning mind, so that none like you has been before you and none like you shall arise after you (1 Kings 3:12 partial)." The Hebrew word demonstrating a wise state of being, "chakam," used to describe what God gave to Solomon means "wise" in the following areas: skillful, shrewd, and prudence.[60] Solomon's business expertise is acknowledged throughout the book of Proverbs, especially on what it means to plan wisely.

Proverbs 15:22
Proverbs 16:3
Proverbs 16:9
Proverbs 19:21
Proverbs 21:5

As a marketplace ambassador for Christ, you have direct access to the wisdom of God to orchestrate, negotiate, and use sound judgment for forthcoming deals and proposals. We just need to exercise humility and ask God for wisdom like Solomon did. James 1:5 tells us, "If any of you lacks wisdom, let him ask God, who gives generously to all without reproach, and it will be given him.

STRATEGY LAYS GROUNDWORK FOR EXECUTION

If you asked Eli Goldratt, author of *The Goal: A Process of Ongoing Improvement*, he'd tell you that the primary aim of a business is to "make money by increasing net profit, while simultaneously increasing return on investment, and simultaneously increasing cash flow."[61] But the burning question for many is, "how do you reach the goal?" That's where a sound strategy comes into play. Dictionary.com defines "strategy" as "a plan, method, or series of maneuvers or stratagems for obtaining a specific goal or result."[62] A good strategy helps move a company towards obtaining its objectives. The strategy journey requires a good bit of discipline because it's very easy to get distracted. In *The 4 Disciplines of Execution*, Chris McChesney, Sean Covey, and Jim Huling lay out four practices to help businesses maintain hyper focus on achieving key targets.[63]

1. **Focus on the Wildly Important.**
2. **Act on the Lead Measures.**
3. **Keep a Compelling Scorecard.**
4. **Create a Cadence of Accountability.**

The absence of rigor around these practices highlight failures such as people not knowing the goal, neglect of value-added activities, unknown success measures, and lack of accountability. The FranklinCovey organization is exceptionally familiar with strategically laying the groundwork for execution, but let's now take a look at execution through the lens of scripture.

EXECUTION

Nehemiah held a royal office (cupbearer to the King) and guided one of the single greatest project management efforts in history, rebuilding the wall of Jerusalem in just 52 days (Nehemiah 6:15). He was incredibly effective because he worked diligently in following God's leading. Carnegie Mellon professor Sean Ammi-rati coined Nehemiah's followership of God as "The Nehemiah Formula (Pray + Plan then Push Forward).[64] I should point out that the outcome here is not just a formula. We can glean a lot from Nehemiah, but the "formula" worked because God led him and supernaturally enabled him. Rather than attempting to repli-cate Nehemiah's success, learn from his response and dedication to God. Professor Ammirati points out, "In the entire 13-chapter Book, Nehemiah deliberately calls out stopping to pray 11 times. I'm sure that he prayed many other times, but the writer takes the time to specifically highlight 11 different times that his trajectory was changed through the power of prayer."[65] **Pillar 1: Pray.**

Pillar 2: Plan. After going to God in prayer, Nehemiah was led by the spirit to concoct a plan. Nehemiah was incredibly strategic and detailed in his planning. First and foremost, he knew his why. As a Hebrew descendant, his heart was broken when his brother informed him that Judah had fallen into exile. See Nehemiah 1:1-3. Out of painful anguish, he set his mind on restoring Judah to its rightful place as a godly, thriving nation (Nehemiah 1:4-11, 2:5). Nehemiah conveyed his plan in a phased approach. Phase 1 consisted of setting a timeline, obtaining lead-ership buy-in, and procuring the necessary resources for successful execution (Nehemiah 2:6-8). In Phase 2, Nehemiah assessed the situation and communicated his vision to the locals in Jerusalem (Nehemiah 2:11-18).

Pillar 3: Push Forward. Once planning was finalized, Nehemiah began executing God's vision for rebuilding the Jerusalem wall. The monstrous effort, full of complexity, was completed in an astounding 52 days (Nehemiah 6:15)! Gates and towers alike. Naturally, when you plan a large effort with policy

altering stakes on the line, opposition occurs. Nehemiah over-
came both political and military threats to finish what he started
(Nehemiah 6:1-2). He led faithfully through crisis and had the
courage to ensure the viability of Jerusalem's future. To push an
initiative and a nation forward, Nehemiah had to be a good
leader and manager.

TAKING INVENTORY

One of the most popular and effective methods for customer
value creation is "lean thinking." The goal of lean thinking is to
amplify customer value while reducing waste. This gets accomplished by companies electing to focus on the "flow" of their
products and or services through the whole value stream. Two
fundamental techniques to go about this operation are assessing
the value of business creation processes and implementing a JIT
(Just-In-Time) inventory system.

When classifying value-added and non-value-added activities,
look for steps in the process that do or don't contribute to the
customer's willingness to pay (Ex. Speed, Quality). Look to elimi-
nate steps that don't affect customer sentiment. One such step
could be reducing the wait time (idle time) in between process
areas. This is where enabling a JIT inventory system can come in
handy. As described in *The Toyota Way*, "JIT means removing, as
much as possible, the inventory used to buffer operations against
problems that may arise in production."[66] An easy example to
follow is building a car. Rather than have spare parts lay around a
factory, parts are ordered to assembly only when a customer
makes a purchase. Taking inventory of resources and people is
important in business, and Jesus even uses this as an example in
teaching.

In Luke 14:28-31, Jesus teaches on the importance of counting
the cost of following Him.

"For which of you, desiring to build a tower, does not first sit
down and count the cost, whether he has enough to complete it?

Otherwise, when he has laid a foundation and is not able to finish, all who see it begin to mock him, saying, 'This man began to build and was not able to finish.' Or what king, going out to encounter another king in war, will not sit down first and deliberate whether he is able with ten thousand to meet him who comes against him with twenty thousand?"

Jesus uses planning principles to make a point while clarifying the sacrifice associated with discipleship:

1. **Can I afford it?**
2. **Do I have enough of the right people?**

King Solomon reiterated some of the same preparation points Jesus touched on back in Proverbs 27:23-24.

"Know well the condition of your flocks, and give attention to your herds, for riches do not last forever; and does a crown endure to all generations?"

As business stewards, regardless of role or title, we are to be found faithful (1 Corinthians 4:2). Faithful planning is comprised of evaluating the goal at hand, ensuring financial viability, and involving people with the right skillsets.

CHAPTER TAKEAWAYS

1. Planning, coupled with diligence, puts the wisdom of God in action for your benefit.
2. "The Nehemiah Formula" = Pray + Plan then Push Forward
3. Faithful planning is comprised of evaluating the goal at hand, ensuring financial viability, and involving people with the right skillset.

HUMAN RESOURCES?

"MASTERS, TREAT YOUR BONDSERVANTS JUSTLY AND FAIRLY, KNOWING THAT YOU ALSO HAVE A MASTER IN HEAVEN."

— COLOSSIANS 4:1

"WHEN PEOPLE GO TO WORK, THEY SHOULDN'T HAVE TO LEAVE THEIR HEARTS AT HOME."

— BETTY BENDER

PEOPLE ARE RESOURCEFUL, NOT RESOURCES

A disheartening travesty in the workplace is how carelessly people treat each other. The quote, "It's not personal. It's just business," gets used as a license to intentionally dehumanize others. On the flip side of things, one can also unintentionally devalue others with his or her vocabulary. Words like resources, human capital, headcount, and butts-in-seats have, unfortunately, become commonplace in HR departments. We must be careful about the words we use to label others. Our words carry lots of weight and power. This point is made clear in scripture.

Proverbs 18:21 "Death and life are in the power of the tongue, and those who love it will eat its fruits."

James 3:3-10 "If we put bits in the mouths of horses so that they obey us, we guide their whole bodies as well. Look at the ships also: though they are so large and are driven by strong winds, they are guided by a very small rudder wherever the will of the pilot directs. So also the tongue is a small member, yet it boasts of great things. How great a forest is set ablaze by such a small fire! And the tongue is a fire, a world of unrighteousness. The tongue is set among our members, staining the whole body, setting on fire the entire course of life, and set on fire by hell. For every kind of beast and bird, of reptile and sea creature, can be tamed and has been tamed by mankind, but no human being can tame the tongue. It is a restless evil, full of deadly poison. With it, we bless our Lord and Father, and with it, we curse people who are made in the likeness of God. From the same mouth come blessing and cursing. My brothers, these things ought not to be so."

The way you treat people, even in the office, is an outward depiction of your soul condition.

DISPLAY EQUITY

While the lifeblood of any business is sales, the foundation of business is people. Dave Ramsey likes to say that "business is easy until people get involved."[67] The leading and hiring of people is the greatest feat any of us can take on. This is why hiring the RIGHT people is such a critical factor in the workplace. The process certainly should not be rushed and needs attention to detail. The culture of a company rides on the kind of people brought into an organization. The Bible outlines the kinds of qualities that make a person stand out amongst the crowd. In 1 Timothy, Paul defines the qualifications for Overseers (aka Pastors) and

Deacons. I think you'll find some of the characteristics in the chapter desirable for both current and future co-workers.

Overseers (Pastors): 1 Timothy 3:1-7

"The saying is trustworthy: If anyone aspires to the office of overseer, he desires a noble task. Therefore an overseer must be above reproach, the husband of one wife, sober-minded, self-controlled, respectable, hospitable, able to teach, not a drunkard, not violent but gentle, not quarrelsome, not a lover of money. He must manage his own household well, with all dignity keeping his children submissive, for if someone does not know how to manage his own household, how will he care for God's church? He must not be a recent convert, or he may become puffed up with conceit and fall into the condemnation of the devil. Moreover, he must be well thought of by outsiders, so that he may not fall into disgrace, into a snare of the devil."

Deacons: 1 Timothy 3:8-13

"Deacons likewise must be dignified, not double-tongued, not addicted to much wine, not greedy for dishonest gain. They must hold the mystery of the faith with a clear conscience. And let them also be tested first; then let them serve as deacons if they prove themselves blameless. Their wives likewise must be dignified, not slanderers, but sober-minded, faithful in all things. Let deacons each be the husband of one wife, managing their children and their own households well. For those who serve well as deacons gain a good standing for themselves and also great confidence in the faith that is in Christ Jesus."

Let's pull out some of the key characteristics from the scriptures:

Exemplary
Dedicated
Focused
Self-Controlled
Respectable

Hospitable
Sober
Gentle
Peaceful
Generous
Steward
A Good Parent
Humble
Reputable
Dignified
Honest
Faithful

Who wouldn't want to hire someone with this kind of character? You can train skills, but you can't teach character.

A good case study on hiring to bring some of this to life is the recruiting process for Dave Ramsey's organization, Ramsey Solutions. I'm not saying his organization is perfect, but they've produced a 700+ employee, $100 million+ company that's been voted ten times as one of the "Best Places to Work in Nashville."[68] After years of poor choices, Dave came up with a 12 step process "to ensure that the right person with the right personality fills the right position."[69]

1. PRAYER Ask God to send who He wants to work with you—and ask Him to keep the crazies away.

2. GET REFERRALS: Post openings on your website and get referrals from your top team members. Don't waste money on advertising.

3. 30-MINUTE DRIVE-BY INTERVIEW: The first step in our interview process is the quick get-to-know-you conversation. It quickly weeds out many candidates.

4. RÉSUMÉ AND REFERENCES: We basically use references

and résumés only for a perfunctory check and as a conversation starter.

5. TESTING TOOLS—THE DISC PROFILE DISC: gives us a quick look at the personality of the person and whether they will fit with a team.

6. DO YOU LIKE THEM?: Basic but true: Don't hire people you wouldn't want to hang out with.

7. DO THEY LIGHT UP?: When you talk about a position, does the person get fired up? If there's no passion, don't offer a job.

8. PERSONAL BUDGET AND MISSION STATEMENT Final candidates must send us their personal budget. We want to make sure they can live on what we would be paying them. Once hired, they must write a personal mission statement to remind them of the new position they accepted is part of living their dream.

9. COMPENSATION CALCULATION, BENEFITS, AND POLICY REVIEW: Let the candidate know all you offer before you hire them. But if they're preoccupied with salary and benefits, it's not the job for them.

10. KEY RESULTS AREA (KRA): Before a job is posted, write a detailed job description (KRA) showing what winning looks like. It's their guide for being successful at your company.

11. SPOUSAL INTERVIEW: As part of the interview process, you and your spouse should go to dinner with the candidate and their spouse. You'll learn more than you ever imagined.

12. 90-DAY PROBATION: Both your company and the new hire are in a trial period for three months. There's little obligation on either side's part.

What if an employee isn't living up to company expectations? Do you fire them immediately? I challenge you to take an approach of course correction before ultimately deciding to terminate. Remember, you worked your tail off to hire great people. More on firing later. Sometimes people go down into valleys they need to be pulled out of. The Bible gives us some good guidelines on reprimanding others.

Matthew 18:15

"If your brother sins against you, go and tell him his fault, between you and him alone. If he listens to you, you have gained your brother."

Proverbs 27:5

"Better is open rebuke than hidden love."

Proverbs 3:12

"for the Lord reproves him whom he loves, as a father the son in whom he delights."

Titus 3:10

"As for a person who stirs up division, after warning him once and then twice, have nothing more to do with him,"

We can extract four helpful insights from the Bible's input on correction:

1. **Be Private**
2. **Be Clear**
3. **Be Reassuring**
4. **Give Multiple Chances**

Privately dealing with an employee protects the employee from public humiliation and the employer from accidentally sending the wrong message to others. Being clear in correcting an employee lets both sides know where each other stands. It's important to be open, honest, and direct. By being reassuring, you show full confidence in an employee that they can change their ways and perform at a high level. Make sure your correction comes from a place of love (well-being). Just as we're to hate the sin and not the sinner, hate the negative behavior and not the person. Lastly, I'll bet you didn't know that the renowned three strikes rule has roots in scripture? Even so, the key is to give multiple chances and leave room for grace before you give an infraction. Make sure the infractions are spelled out clearly so that they don't catch anyone off guard. Craft an explicit vision of what both progress and regression look like. Sometimes, however, you just need to move on from a person when they are unwilling to change.

Naturally, when we're referring to someone unwilling to change, we're talking about terminating or firing them. I'd like to shed some light on the firing process. Just because a situation doesn't work out in your or the company's favor, we have no excuse to allow it to impact our faith walk. Yes, we're human beings who have emotions. No, we're not to hold grudges against employers or employees because of our biased thoughts and feelings. The Bible is very clear on grudges and the impact they have.

James 5:9 NKJV

"Do not grumble against one another, brethren, lest ye be condemned: Behold, the Judge is standing at the door."[70]

Mark 11:25 NLT

"But when you are praying, first forgive anyone you are holding a grudge against, so that your Father in heaven will forgive your sins, too."[71]

Not holding grudges covers the essence of firing, now we're going to talk about firing in form. Legendary Ford CEO Alan Mulally had perhaps the most out of the box thinking on termination. A widely known story within corporate ranks is how Mulally responded to a prominent member of his leadership team when he chose not to show up to an important strategy meeting. Mulally confronted him and asked why he wasn't in attendance. The gentleman explained that he was busy and couldn't commit to the weekly cadence. Mulally smiled and simply responded, "that's okay." The executive was both relieved and confused with a response of "really?" Mulally, still smiling, said, "Yeah. We can still be friends. But you can't work here. It's up to you."[72] There was no yelling, profanity, threats, bitterness, or malice from Alan Mulally. During his tenure at Ford, he very rarely fired anyone. Most people fired themselves.

People are the building blocks of an organization. This statement cannot merely be lip service. It must be demonstrated. There's a wide spectrum of factors that influence employee satisfaction, including (but not limited to) compensation, promotion opportunities, and leader confidence, to name a few. Unfortunately, high turnover rates, low employee satisfaction, and lack of employee engagement have been the byproduct of ambition, greed, and selfishness in the workplace. The Bible is the perfect equalizer to speak into how people (employees) should be treated.

Compensation

The Bible gives examples of treating people in your employment fairly.

Colossians 4:1 – Fair Treatment

"Masters, treat your bondservants justly and fairly, knowing that you also have a Master in heaven."

Deuteronomy 24:15 – Timely Pay

"You shall give him his wages on the same day, before the sun sets (for he is poor and counts on it), lest he cry against you to the Lord, and you be guilty of sin."

Jeremiah 22:13 – Integrity

"Woe to him who builds his house by unrighteousness, and his upper rooms by injustice, who makes his neighbor serve him for nothing and does not give him his wages,"

Promotion

The Bible states that God is the true overseer of promotion and that it comes from displays of *talent*, *skill*, and *service*.

Exodus 31:1-5

"The Lord said to Moses, 'See, I have called by name Bezalel the son of Uri, son of Hur, of the tribe of Judah, and I have filled him with the Spirit of God, with ability and intelligence, with knowledge and all craftsmanship, to devise artistic designs, to work in gold, silver, and bronze, in cutting stones for setting, and in carving wood, to work in every craft."

Proverbs 22:29

"Do you see a man skillful in his work? He will stand before kings; he will not stand before obscure men."

1 Peter 5:6

"Humble yourselves, therefore, under the mighty hand of God so that at the proper time he may exalt you,"

Leader Confidence

The employer/employee or manager/direct report relationship often gets portrayed in the workplace as adversarial and depicted as a breeding ground for one-upmanship. Not so when it comes to scripture. The Bible lays out a synergistic relationship where both parties take a godly posture towards and a reliance on each other.

Ephesians 6:5-9

"Bondservants, obey your earthly masters with fear and trembling, with a sincere heart, as you would Christ, not by way of eye-service, as people-pleasers, but as bondservants of Christ, doing the will of God from the heart, rendering service with a good will as to the Lord and not to man, knowing that whatever good anyone does, this he will receive back from the Lord, whether he is a bondservant or is free. Masters, do the same to them, and stop your threatening, knowing that he who is both their Master and yours is in heaven, and that there is no partiality with him."

Let's pull out some of the suggested behavioral attributes between bondservant/master and how they might apply in the employee/employer relationship.

Bondservant (Employee/Direct Report):
Respect

Sincerity
Authenticity

Master (Employer/Manager):
Respect
Sincerity
Authenticity
Gracious

Eb Ikonne, a Senior Vice President at Cox Automotive, describes this kind of environment where everyone can thrive as "joy at work."[73]

Partiality does not reflect the love of Jesus Christ in the workplace. Instead, it influences a company through the conniving practice of office politics. We'll revisit politics later on in this chapter.

The Bible exposes 3 points about favoritism:

It does not reflect God's character.
It is discouraged.
It is sin.

Romans 2:11
"For God shows no partiality."
James 2:1
"My brothers, show no partiality as you hold the faith in our Lord Jesus Christ, the Lord of glory."
James 2:8-9
"If you really fulfill the royal law according to the Scripture, "You shall love your neighbor as yourself," you are doing well. But if you show partiality, you are committing sin and are convicted by the law as transgressors."

Women are an integral part of God's plan for business. The Father has granted them intuition, discernment, and extraordinary attention to detail. However, because of sinful influences in the workplace, women have been abused and oppressed by sexual harassment and male chauvinism. This is not the way God's daughters, whether entrepreneurial, managerial, or individual contributors, are to be treated. As a Father adores his baby girl, so Christ lavishes His love upon women. The Bible regularly features female metaphors to symbolize God's love and admiration for His people.

Zephaniah 3:14 – Israel's Restoration

"Sing aloud, O daughter of Zion; shout, O Israel! Rejoice and exult with all your heart, O daughter of Jerusalem!"

Isaiah 66:13 – Jerusalem Rejoices

"As one whom his mother comforts, so I will comfort you; you shall be comforted in Jerusalem."

John 12:15 – Jesus' Triumphal Entry

"Fear not, daughter of Zion; behold, your king is coming, sitting on a donkey's colt!"

Men, if God feels this way about women (which He does), then what prevents us from having the same love for and admiration towards them? Men, I'm going to be frank. Many (not all) failures of the enterprise are due to our selfishness. God designed the earth to be jointly ruled and cultivated with women through business (Genesis 1:27-28). Ladies, you don't have to prove your worth, just take heart in what Christ Jesus has graced you to accomplish. The world demands that you live, act, think, and dress a certain way. God does not. Remember, you are in the world, not of the world, which makes you ladies, out of this world!

Some of the most impactful women in business modern-day include names like Oprah Winfrey (Creator of OWN – The Oprah Winfrey Network) and Sarah Blakely (Founder of SPANX). But did you also know the Bible documented many women who held high offices and were savvy with their businesses and finances? Even in times of persecution, exile, and famine!

Esther was Queen of Persia.

Esther 2:17

"the king loved Esther more than all the women, and she won grace and favor in his sight more than all the virgins, so that he set the royal crown on her head and **made her queen** instead of Vashti."

Deborah was the first and only female judge of Israel.

Judges 4:4-5

"Now Deborah, a prophetess, the wife of Lappidoth, **was judging Israel** at that time. She used to sit under the palm of Deborah between Ramah and Bethel in the hill country of Ephraim, and **the people of Israel came up to her for her judgment.**"

Lydia was a merchant of Purple goods.

Acts 16:14

"One who heard us was a woman named Lydia, from the city of Thyatira, **a seller of purple goods**, who was a worshipper of God. The Lord opened her heart to pay attention to what was said by Paul."

Phoebe was a deaconess and a financial supporter of the Gospel.

Romans 16:1-2

"I commend to you our sister Phoebe, a **servant** of the church at Cenchreae, that you may welcome her in the Lord in a way worthy of the saints, and help her in whatever she may need from you, for she has been a **patron** of many and of myself as well."

Priscilla (Prisca) was a tentmaker.

Acts 18:1-3

"After this Paul left Athens and went to Corinth. And he found a Jew named Aquila, a native of Pontus, recently come from Italy with his wife Priscilla, because Claudius had commanded all the Jews to leave Rome. And he went to see them, and because he was of the same trade, he stayed with them and worked, for they were **tentmakers** by trade."

Shiphrah and Puah were midwives.

Exodus 1:15-17

"Then the king of Egypt said to the Hebrew **midwives**, one of whom was named Shiphrah and the other Puah, "When you serve as midwife to the Hebrew women and see them on the birthstool, if it is a son, you shall kill him, but if it is a daughter, she shall live." But the midwives feared God and did not do as the king of Egypt commanded them, but let the male children live."

The Virtuous Woman was the owner of multiple businesses.

Proverbs 31:13, 16, 18-19, 24

"She seeks wool and flax and works with willing hands."

"She considers a field and buys it; with the fruit of her hands, she plants a vineyard."

"She perceives that her merchandise is profitable. Her lamp does not go out at night."

"She puts her hands to the distaff, and her hands hold the spindle."

"She makes linen garments and sells them; she delivers sashes to the merchant."

We must continue to support, encourage, train, coach, teach, and mentor women in business so they can accomplish what God has called them to do. Rock on, ladies!

CELEBRATE PEOPLE

It's very easy to get caught up in the mundane nature of work if we're not careful. Routines are great for forming habits, but not so much when it comes to lauding people. We become so desensitized to the great work going on around us that we detach from people and purpose. It's important to celebrate others as well as enjoying yourself when attaining individual milestones. The Bible gives some healthy considerations in both of these areas.

Romans 13:7 – Commend Others

"Pay to all what is owed to them: taxes to whom taxes are owed, revenue to whom revenue is owed, respect to whom respect is owed, **honor to whom honor is owed.**"

Psalm 128:2 – Enjoy The Fruit of Your Labor

"You shall **eat the fruit of the labor of your hands**; you shall be blessed, and it shall be well with you."

If you're in the camp of people that don't believe it's that big of a deal to appreciate others, you're in for a rude awakening. In their book *The 5 Languages of Appreciation In The Workplace*, Dr. Gary Chapman and Dr. Paul White conducted research that revealed "64 percent of Americans who leave their jobs say they do so because they don't feel appreciated."[74] Appreciation isn't about money. There are more layers under the onion for each worker. An appreciated employee is an engaged employee. Chapman and White have actually classified workplace appreciation into five distinct categories they call "languages."

Appreciation Language #1: Words of Affirmation

- Communicating a positive message to another person.

Appreciation Language #2: Quality Time

- Giving a person your focused attention.

Appreciation Language #3: Acts of Service

- Lending a helping hand to a colleague.

Appreciation Language #4: Tangible Gifts

- Giving the right gift to someone who values the reward.

Appreciation Language #5: Physical Touch

- Appropriate, meaningful contact based on specific situations.

Above is a brief overview of "what" the five languages of appreciation are, but let's explore the "why" behind them. Chapman and White found that "only 12 percent of employees reported leaving for more money, while 88 percent of employees state they leave for reasons other than money."[75] They further uncovered that "the reasons most often cited by departing employees were more psychological in nature—including not feeling trusted or valued."[76] The point they are making is that appreciation has an ROI. They highlight five benefits of choosing to focus on building a culture of appreciation:[77]

1. **Express genuine appreciation to co-workers and staff — even on a tight budget.**
2. **Increase loyalty with the employees and volunteers in your organization.**
3. **Reduce cynicism and create a more positive work environment.**
4. **Improve your ability to show appreciation for difficult colleagues.**
5. **Convey the language of physical touch in appropriate ways.**

The five languages of appreciation were derived from Dr. Chapman's five love languages. Everything comes back to love. There must be a relentless pursuit of love in the marketplace because it demonstrates the example of Jesus Christ.

ELIMINATE POLITICS

We just barely started to scratch the surface of office politics earlier in the chapter. Depending on your work environment, you may feel like there's more going on behind the scenes than what's advertised. Better yet, beyond feelings, you may have witnessed the secret, underhanded schemes that men and women selfishly devise. A culture of politics is problematic for multiple reasons. One, it creates division in the form of an "us vs. them" turf war. An inner circle of people with access to information and benefits, and a seemingly outer circle of people controlled by fear. Secondly, politics foster a climate of distrust. A lack of trust will always cripple the leadership of an organization. People can't believe in a north star vision if they can't trust the people around them. Thirdly, politics create a breeding ground for gossip. Gossip is like a lethal coronavirus that spreads out of control. Its symptoms are highly contagious and have ruined many an organization.

BEWARE OF GOSSIP

One surefire way to diminish the impact of politics is to deal with gossip head-on. God takes a strong stance against gossip because He doesn't stand for anything that causes strife. However, to deal with gossip, we have to understand its nature.

Gossip is tempting.

Proverbs 18:8

"The words of a whisperer are like delicious morsels; they go down into the inner most parts of the body."

Gossip is learned behavior.

1 Timothy 5:13

"Besides that, **they learn** to be idlers, going about from house to house, and not only idlers, but also **gossips** and busybodies, saying what they should not."

Gossip travels with a gang of evil.

2 Corinthians 12:20

"For I fear that perhaps when I come I may find you not as I wish, and that you may find me not as you wish—that perhaps there may be quarreling, jealousy, anger, hostility, slander, **gossip**, conceit, and disorder."

Dave Ramsey defines gossip as "when you have a problem, and you yap about it to someone who can't help you fix it."[78] Everyone in an organization is a defender and keeper of the culture. It's a shared responsibility, not a role responsibility. Gossip is toxic waste that pollutes the very fabric of a company unless you step up and do your part. Here are two simple tactics you can apply to help you clean up company gossip:

1. **Don't Participate** – Refuse to be a middleman. Let people know that you don't take part in talking behind people's backs or discussing unsanctioned topics. You might not be liked by some for doing this, but you will be respected.

2. **Take It To Leadership** – Dare the parties involved to take the issue to management. This accomplishes two things: one, it helps reveal the person's true intent for spreading the gossip, and two, it puts the ball in the other person's court to take action.

SLICE THE SILO STRUCTURE

The next topic we'll discuss is what I consider a "blind spot" in many organizations. Believe it or not, leaders can build politics into how they run a company. Companies traditionally divide their labor structure into distinct departments (HR, Finance, Sales, Operations, IT, etc.). Division of labor? Company verticals? Do any of these phrases sound familiar? Wherever you have silos in your organization (especially under command & control leadership), there exists the opportunity for competing priorities.

An example of this would be a sales team selling products and services with no regard for operations. Imagine a sales group overpromising due to outrageous sale quotas. Consider the pressure that practice would put on operations to frantically "keep the lights on." While I've used a fictional example, a real-life story came eerily close to this.

Wells Fargo bank was exposed in a major corporate scandal where they "were discovered to have opened millions of unauthorized accounts and issued millions of unauthorized cards to meet punishing sales goals, on pain of termination."[79] This unethical behavior was found to have been in place for almost 14 years, possibly dating back to 2002. Public humiliation, job loss, and corporate trials all due to corrupt leadership, culture, and a heinous sales organization. Eric Ries (The Lean Startup) would offer the following take on Wells Fargo's corporate blunder: "the criticism should be aimed at senior executives who failed to design a supportive system in which to operate and innovate."[80]

Let me be clear about my intent. I'm not attempting to prescribe companies on how they "should be" set up. What I will touch on, however, is "why" the structure of a company matters. Business, God's way, promotes a spirit of collaboration, transparency, and service, not individualism, ambiguity, and disservice. Jesus Christ established a body that did the former: the Church. With His sacrifice on the cross, He tore down the bureaucratic operation of the Pharisees and Sadducees. No matter your opinion about the current state of the Church, its humble origins (documented in the book of Acts) were a non-political assembly of people meeting the needs of others. Take a look in the book of Acts at what they were capable of with no hidden agendas (Acts 2:42-47):

Devotion (Acts 2:42)
Unity (Acts 2:44)
Community (Acts 2:45)
Generosity (Acts 2:46)
Growth (Acts 2:47)

Perhaps one of the most radical cases of a company choosing a non-traditional operating structure is online shoe retailer

Zappos. Zappos CEO Tony Hsieh set up what is known as a "holacracy." A holacracy is "a new way of structuring and running your organization that replaces the conventional management hierarchy. Instead of operating top-down, power is distributed throughout the organization – giving individuals and teams freedom while staying aligned to the organization's purpose."[81] I mention Zappos neither as a way for you to benchmark your company structure, nor to debate management theory, but instead to capture the spirit of what they were going after: a purpose-filled company free of "pecking order politics." Hsieh understood his role in constructing the design of Zappos. Leaders "know the way, go the way, and show the way."[82]

Politics keep companies from reaching their highest potential. Politics stifle innovation. Politics create a culture of corporate maneuvering to get things done. None of these are outcomes God desires for business. He longs for a marketplace full of companies focused on spreading love and demonstrating faithfulness.

CHAPTER TAKEAWAYS

1. Gossip is toxic waste that pollutes the very fabric of a company unless you step up and do your part.
2. An appreciated employee is an engaged employee.
3. Business, God's way, promotes a spirit of collaboration, transparency, and service, not individualism, ambiguity, and disservice.

TEAMWORK MAKES THE DREAM WORK

"FOR JUST AS THE BODY IS ONE AND HAS MANY MEMBERS, AND ALL THE MEMBERS OF THE BODY, THOUGH MANY, ARE ONE BODY, SO IT IS WITH CHRIST."

— 1 CORINTHIANS 12:12

"TEAMING IS A PROCESS OF BRINGING TOGETHER SKILLS AND IDEAS FROM DISPARATE AREAS TO PRODUCE SOMETHING NEW—SOMETHING THAT NO INDIVIDUAL, OR EVEN A GROUP IN ONE AREA OF EXPERTISE, COULD DO ALONE."

— AMY EDMONDSON

BECOME AN IDEAL TEAM PLAYER

Everybody loves a team player. This is the kind of person who lights up the room when they walk in. He or she has an infectious personality, undeniable influence, and earned trustworthiness. Team players are present in every environment imaginable.

The workplace, the military, families, and athletics. One of the most selfless team players out there is none other than Steph Curry of the NBA's Golden State Warriors. Steph Curry is a 3-time NBA champion, 2-time NBA Most Valuable Player, and the only voted unanimous Most Valuable Player in NBA history. Yet, he would tell you that these individual accolades are not what make him extraordinary.

The secret sauce is written in Steph Curry's Twitter handle (@StephenCurry30): **Believer**. Husband to @ayeshacurry, father to Riley, Ryan and Canon, son, brother. Golden State Warriors guard. Davidson Wildcat. Philippians 4:13 #IWILL[83] In a special mini-series on Facebook, Curry responded to a question from the interviewer about the intentionality of his social media account: "I put believer first, because that is supposed to be the roots of everything I do as a believer, as a husband, as a father, and on down from there."[84] Christ leads with love. Curry puts Christ first. Since Curry is a follower of Christ, he leads with love by being a relational leader and selfless teammate to others.

Patrick Lencioni, pioneer of the organizational health movement, ranks Steph Curry as one of his three model "ideal team players" along with former Ford CEO Allan Mulally and fictional character Woody from Disney's *Toy Story*.[85] In his book *The Ideal Team Player*, Lencioni teaches us how to identify and nurture the three vital virtues of being humble, hungry, and smart.

BE HUMBLE

Patrick Lencioni believes "humility is the single greatest and most indispensable attribute of being a team player." He goes on to profile humility in his book (The Ideal Team Player) by pointing out seven distinct behaviors that humble people demonstrate:[86]

1. **They lack excessive ego**
2. **The lack of concern about status**

3. **They are quick to point out the contributions of others**
4. **They are slow to seek attention for their own contribution**
5. **They share credit**
6. **They emphasize team over self**
7. **They define success collectively rather than individually**

If humility is the hero of the story, there has to be a villain. That enemy's name would be arrogance. People often get away with a lack of humility in the workplace because they're not held accountable for their conduct. You can "smell" the funk of a prideful person from miles away. Arrogance is an intangible killer that brings down morale and discourages collaboration. Overcoming the fear of conflict is a major obstacle that keeps people from addressing a prideful person's attitude.

Lencioni asserts that there are two kinds of people who lack humility: the "overtly arrogant" (as discussed above), and those who "lack self-confidence (but are generous and positive)."[87] The latter can many times go undetected. These individuals struggle with acknowledging their own self-worth. They tend to "go along to get along" and not speak out when solicited for feedback or ideas. Believe it or not, both of these kinds of people have a common thread between them: a rotted root of insecurity. Lencioni summarizes their self-doubt this way: "Insecurity makes some people project overconfidence, and others discount their own talents. And while these types are not equal when it comes to creating problems on a team, they each diminish performance."[88]

Humility is not something organizational psychologists or savvy businessmen cooked up in the kitchen. It is an attribute epitomized by God and to be emulated by His children. According to Blue Letter Bible, the word "humble" appears forty times within thirty-nine verses in the English Standard Translation (ESV) across the following books: Exodus, Deuteronomy, Judges, 2 Samuel, 2 Chronicles, Ezra, Psalm, Proverbs, Isaiah, Jeremiah, Ezekiel, Daniel, Zephaniah, Zechariah, Matthew, Luke, 2 Corinthians, James, 1 Peter.[89]

Two scriptures, in particular, highlight how God responds to people who exhibit humility.

James 4:6

"But he gives more grace. Therefore it says, 'God opposes the proud, but gives **grace** to the humble.'"

1 Peter 5:6

"Humble yourselves, therefore, under the mighty hand of God so at the proper time he may **exalt** you,"

Here are our two key takeaways from living a life of humility:

1. **Grace is given to the humble**
2. **The humble will be elevated in due time**

For a deeper characterization of humility, consider the story of Joseph. Joseph went on a journey from safety in the household of his father Jacob, to being sold into slavery by his jealous brothers, to being falsely accused of an affair by Potiphar's wife, then to jail, finally ending up as second in command of Egypt under Pharaoh. What a story filled with joy and sorrow! But more than that, what a display of faith in God. Joseph never waned from the mission of serving God and serving people. Join me in reviewing Joseph's noble displays of humility in the midst of adversity.

Joseph interpreted two prisoners' dreams while imprisoned.

Genesis 40:8

"They said to him, "We have had dreams, and there is no one to interpret them." And Joseph said to them, "Do not interpretations belong to God?" Please tell them to me."

Joseph refused to sleep with Potiphar's wife while watching over his household.

Genesis 39:7-9

"And after a time his master's wife cast her eyes on Joseph and said, 'Lie with me.' But he refused and said to his master's wife, 'Behold, because of me my master has no concern about anything in the house, and he has put everything that he has in my charge. He is not greater in this house than I am, nor has he kept back anything from me except you, because you are his wife. How then can I do this great wickedness and sin against God?'"

Joseph interpreted Pharaoh's dream while imprisoned.

Genesis 41:14-16

"Then Pharaoh sent and called Joseph, and they quickly brought him out of the pit. And when he had shaved himself and changed his clothes, he came in before Pharaoh. And Pharaoh said to Joseph, "I have had a dream, and there is no one who can interpret it. I have heard it said of you that when you hear a dream, you can interpret it." Joseph answered Pharaoh, "It is not in me; God will give Pharaoh a favorable answer."

Joseph guided Egypt through famine even though he was a foreigner (Hebrew).

Genesis 41:56-57

"So, when the famine had spread over all the land, Joseph opened all the storehouses and sold to the Egyptians, for the famine was severe in the land of Egypt. Moreover, all the earth came to Egypt to Joseph to buy grain, because the famine was severe over all the earth."

Joseph had mercy on his brothers when he could have taken revenge.

Genesis 45:5-8

"And now do not be distressed or angry with yourselves because you sold me here, for God sent me before you to preserve life. For the famine has been in the land these two years, and there are yet five years in which there will be neither plowing nor harvest. And God sent me before you to preserve for you a remnant on earth, and to keep alive for you many survivors. So it was not you who sent me here, but God. He has made me a father to Pharaoh, and lord of all his house and ruler over all the land of Egypt."

In a corporate sense, you could say Joseph was blackballed by his teams (family, Egypt). Though Joseph was wronged by both his family and the country he served (Egypt), because of his dedication and humble character, he was raised to a position of authority to aid them in the time of crisis. This is God's irony in motion.

BE HUNGRY

The second virtue Lencioni discusses in his book is hunger. People with a strong sense of hunger resemble "worker bees." They always have a desire to do more for the organization. Hungry people, as championed by Lencioni, "almost never have to be pushed by a manager to work harder because they are self-motivated and diligent."[90] Hungry people generally have a good sense of "why" they're doing the work they're doing. They also have a natural bent for possessing great work ethic. Like any quality, though, hunger has a light side and a shadow side to it.

Hungry people who venture too deep into the shadows could start to display two notable warning signs: workaholism and selfishness. For hungry people, it's important to set boundaries and timeboxes. An example of a boundary would be turning off the work phone or not checking work email once at home. A great story about timeboxing came from a sermon I heard by Pastor Jeff Hidden of Victory Church in Acworth, GA.[91] Early in his marriage, he would spend hours at home preparing Sunday sermons. When this habit became obsessive, his wife Pippa would come into his home office promptly at 5 p.m. and sit on his lap, purposely blocking his view until he shut his laptop. She understood the need for people to get a good message on Sunday, but she also knew her husband's ability to shepherd the church effectively meant having a fruitful marriage. Without measures such as these in place, answering the beckoning call of work goes unimpeded. Additionally, the frequency of work can cause one's motives to be questioned. Is time away from your family and friends worth the organizational call to action? A good filter to run a hungry person's ambition through is a question I once heard at a Souly Business retreat: Are you ***driven*** to do what you're doing, or are you ***called*** to do it? [92] Remember, striving is surviving, but being faithful is sweet like maple. Food for thought, Mr. or Mrs. Hungry. Food...for...thought.

The Bible honors hard work but admonishes selfish ambition. The difference between God's call to action and the world's is love. The world is only concerned with satisfying the pride of life and the lust of the flesh. Michael Douglas' character Gordon Gekko in the movie *Wall Street* spoke for the world when he said, "...Greed, for lack of a better word, is good."[93] Two verses of scripture tell us nothing good happens when selfish ambition is the catalyst of an endeavor.

Philippians 2:3

"Do nothing from selfish **ambition** or conceit, but in humility count others more significant than yourselves."

James 3:16

"For where jealousy and selfish **ambition** exist, there will be disorder and every vile practice."

Two key points here. One, selfish ambition is an incorrect motivation. Two, selfish ambition, accompanied by jealousy, produces chaos and immorality. So, what is the proper motivation and outcome God desires? Part two of Philippians 2:3 tells us it's humility. There's that "h" word again! When we work (aka hunger) from a place of humility and seeking God, God teaches us his ways (Psalm 25:9).

BE SMART

The third and final virtue Lencioni informs us about is "smart." But it's not what you think. To be smart is to have people skills. We're not talking about IQ (intelligence quotient) but rather EQ (emotional quotient). EQ refers to emotional intelligence. More on EQ shortly. Lencioni mentions that "Smart people just have good judgment and intuition around the subtleties of group dynamics and the impact of their words and actions."[94] This "judgment and intuition" Lencioni speaks of can be broken down further. Psychologist Daniel Goleman pinpointed a set of five skills that "enable the best leaders to maximize their own and their followers' performance."[95] These are known as the EI (emotional intelligence) skills:[96]

Self-awareness – knowing one's strengths, weaknesses, drives, values, and impact on others

Self-regulation – controlling or redirecting disruptive impulses and moods

Motivation – relishing achievement for its own sake

Empathy – understanding other people's emotional makeup

Social Skills – building rapport with others to move them in desired directions

Now don't be deceived. Smart isn't the apex attribute of Lencioni's three. That title belongs to humility. Smart, sure enough, has its dark side. Some of the highest-rated smart people in history have used this superpower for evil in the form of manipulation. Many examples of this can be found in scripture.

Sanballat, Tobiah, and Geshem politically plot against Nehemiah

Nehemiah 6:1-14

Judas Iscariot's false plea for generosity to Jesus

John 12:4-6

A circle of deceit between Jacob and Laban

Genesis 29, 30, 31

In each of these cases, a strong understanding of people and situational awareness were strengths of the deceivers. Both of these characteristics are inherently good. But the "people person" power went sour because of self-centeredness.

TOGETHER EVERYONE ACHIEVES MORE

To become a good team, you must first have good teammates. The first part of this chapter focused on becoming an ideal team player. Now that we know what a quality team member looks like, we can now dissect the "teamwork" and "teaming" aspects of a team. Consider the T.E.A.M acronym: Together Everyone Achieves More. Each one of those words is significant in their own right. A team that is together is a team that is unified. The word "everyone" signifies the unique contribution of each individual. Achievement highlights the goal the team is going after. The word "more" indicates the impact a team makes over one person attempting to do something alone. The strength of the pack compared to the lone ranger is taught in more detail by John Maxwell's Law of Significance.

THE LAW OF SIGNIFICANCE

In John Maxwell's *17 Indisputable Laws of Teamwork*, he established what was known as The Law of Significance: One Is Too Small A Number To Achieve Greatness.[97] One person, though gifted and talented, is limited by the impact that he or she can provide. I'm not referring to ability. Rather, I'm alluding to capacity. Take the military, for example. A highly trained Navy Seal can take out several enemies individually because of skilled marksmanship and lethal hand to hand combat training. But when you get a whole team full of Special Forces fighting together as one unit, look out enemy!

Earlier in the book, we spoke of conducting business God's way in the spirit of unity. One of the ways we can "unite" within a corporate setting is through the effective formation and functioning of teams. God himself is a multiplier and used the principle of multiplication to ripple his plan through the ages. God accomplished this through team types. Let's take a peek at some of the great team-ups in scripture.

The 3 Hebrew Boys: The three Hebrew boys (*Shadrach, Meshach, and Abednego*) exercised great faith by standing up to King Nebuchadnezzar and refusing to worship the golden statue. God rescued them in the fire, and they were promoted to the highest office in the royal court.

The 12 Apostles: Hand-picked by Jesus Christ, these twelve men would carry the gospel across the globe: *Peter, James, John, Andrew, Bartholomew, James, Judas (later replaced by Matthias), Jude, Matthew, Philip, Simon The Zealot, Thomas*

The 12 Tribes of Israel: The 12 tribes of Israel ventured into God's "Promise Land" and established the Nation of Israel. *Levi, Zebulon, Gad, Benjamin, Simeon, Issachar, Naphtali, Joseph, Reuben, Judah, Dan, Asher*

Gideon's 300: Pop culture may know of King Leonidas' leading of 300 Spartans at The Battle of Thermopylae, but God had his hand on Gideon, The Mighty Man of Valor, and his 300 while fighting and defeating the Midianites.

The Power of 2: While the Bible references many team examples, the power of 2 was a special team relationship that God used to bring salvation, mentorship, and discipleship.

Moses & Joshua – Led Israel out of captivity into the Promise Land

Elijah & Elisha – Helped guide and restore Israel during a time of wicked leadership

David & Jonathan – Produced the greatest example of friendship and brotherhood against all odds

Paul & Timothy – A spiritual father/son relationship that established the roots of Christian mentorship in the church

Aquila & Priscilla – A primary example of husband and wife serving and working together unto the Lord

The Bible speaks with fervor about what's possible when two come together in the name of Christ:

Agreement - Matthew 18:19-20

"Again I say to you, if **two** of you agree on earth about anything they ask, it will be done for them by my Father in heaven. For where **two** or three are gathered in my name, there am I among them."

Resourcefulness - Ecclesiastes 4:9-12

"**Two** are better than one, because they have a good reward for their toil. For if they fall, one will lift up his fellow. But woe to him who is alone when he falls and has not another to lift him up! Again, if **two** lie together, they keep warm, but how can one keep warm alone? And though a man might prevail against one who is alone, **two** will withstand him-a threefold cord is not quickly broken."

Who wouldn't want a team united in agreement and rich with resourcefulness? Teamwork makes God's dream, the hope for humanity, work.

TEAM OR GROUP OF WORKING INDIVIDUALS?

By now, we know what it means to be an ideal team player. We even know the powerful outcomes that teamwork produces. But what about the process of forming a team? How does a group actually band together? Would you immediately recognize a team if you walked into an office? We'll begin with the theory designed by Dr. Bruce Tuckman called Tuckman's Model. Tuckman's Model examines the progression of team development and team performance across a spectrum of four stages:[98]

Forming – Learning about each other
Storming – Challenging each other
Norming – Functioning together

Performing – Operating as one

Biblically speaking, one team type example in particular that grows through similar stages is a marriage. Marriage is God's fundamental unit of family. Upon looking at Tuckman's model, let me say this: the way God designed marriage is for man and woman to spiritually join together as one from inception. However, on the practical side of things, consider the seasons of the year. Think about how the elements of each season are different. Just as teams mature and progress through the stages of Tuckman's Model, so too does a marriage adapt over time. An exploration of Tuckman's model is important because it heightens the awareness of why you simply can't throw a group of people together to get something done. They need time and proper conditions to succeed.

We now know the stages that a team progresses through, but what about the conditions for success? Psychologist, J. Richard Hackman identified what he called "essential features of real teams."[99] According to Hackman, "Real work teams in organizations have four features: a team task, clear boundaries, clearly specified authority to manage their own work processes, and membership stability over time."[100]

The perfect team type to analyze Hackman's essential features with is the Church. The collective team task for the Church is the Great Commission (Matthew 28:19) given by Jesus Christ. The boundary that the Church functions within is the commandment "to love one another (John 13:34)." The authority of the Church is headed by Jesus Christ (Ephesians 1:22-23), but he allows its management to fall under the offices of the fivefold ministry: Pastors, Teachers, Apostles, Prophets, and Evangelists (Ephesians 4:11-12). While membership at an individual local church can fluctuate (for any number of reasons), the Body of Christ (Church) goes forth spreading the gospel in victory over darkness (Matthew 16:18). An examination of Hackman's essential features matters because the effectiveness of teams cannot be fully realized without these critical pre-conditions. Otherwise, without them, you don't have true teams; you merely have groups of working individuals.

CHAPTER TAKEAWAYS

1. To become a good team, you must first have good teammates.
2. Be humble. Be hungry. Be smart (people smart).
3. One of the ways we can "unite" within a corporate setting is through the formation of teams.

LEAN INTO CONFLICT

"SO IF YOU ARE OFFERING YOUR GIFT AT THE ALTAR AND THERE REMEMBER THAT YOUR BROTHER HAS SOMETHING AGAINST YOU, LEAVE YOUR GIFT THERE BEFORE THE ALTAR AND GO. FIRST BE RECONCILED TO YOUR BROTHER, AND THEN COME AND OFFER YOUR GIFT."

— MATTHEW 5:23-24

"...THE FEAR OF CONFLICT IS ALMOST ALWAYS A SIGN OF PROBLEMS"

— PATRICK LENCIONI

DYSFUNCTION PREVENTS PROGRESS

One of the greatest NBA rosters ever constructed was the 2003-2004 Los Angeles Lakers. That team oozed talent, having assembled four Hall of Famers: the late Kobe Bryant, Shaquille O'Neal, Karl Malone, and Gary Payton. They were the league favorites, and many considered it a foregone conclusion that LA would win the NBA Finals. The team did, in fact, make it to the NBA Finals that season, but they were dealt a crushing series loss at the hands of the Detroit Pistons. While Detroit had a special cinderella year and beat the Lakers pretty handily, it was really the culmination of season-long dysfunction that ultimately derailed Los Angeles.

Earlier that year, Kobe Bryant and Shaquille O'Neal began one of the most highly profiled public feuds in sports media history. Years later, the two would reconcile, but their issues no question damaged the team's progress and prevented an opportunity to win an unprecedented four championships in five years. Dysfunction stifles the progress of any organization, no matter how seemingly invincible. In one more ode to Patrick Lencioni, we'll break down the consequences of not dealing with dysfunction properly.

ABSENCE OF TRUST

In Patrick Lencioni's *The Five Dysfunctions of A Team*, he talks through five hazards that derail even the best of teams. The first of those is an **Absence of Trust**. Trust is of the utmost importance. It's the sturdy foundation that a team depends on. Said best by Stephen M. R. Covey, "everything moves at the speed of trust."[101] Where there are low levels of trust, there is also a lack of openness and vulnerability.

Proverbs 3:5-6 tells us to "Trust in the Lord with all your heart, and do not lean on your own understanding. In all your ways acknowledge him, and he will make straight your paths." This passage provides both the symptom of and the cure to lacking trust.

Symptom:

Self-Reliance

Cure:

Surrender

If your team is going to evolve successfully, you must stop

relying on your own knowledge and start surrendering to God's omnipotent wisdom.

Action: In your time of devotion, pray and ask God what's preventing your team from surrendering company decisions to him.

FEAR OF CONFLICT

Moving up the hierarchy of dysfunction, **Fear of Conflict** is the next culprit. The fear of conflict is a lot like the medical condition gangrene. Gangrene, as defined by WebMD, "is the death of body tissues, usually due to a lack of blood supply, especially in the legs and feet."[102] When nobody is willing to engage in healthy conflict, the organization slowly dies and withers away. Healthy debate and disagreement are a natural "blood supply" needed to analyze ideas and make difficult decisions.

In Jonah chapter 1, we find Jonah, a prophet of God, fleeing God's request of him to warn the city of Nineveh about their evil ways. He sailed at sea with a group of travelers, but the boat he was on suddenly experienced a great wind from God. Because of Jonah's fear and unwillingness to confront the city of Nineveh, he put the other sailors' lives at stake with a risk of drowning. Fear of conflict doesn't just hurt you; it affects others around you.

Action: In your time of devotion, pray and ask God how to face your fears and address conflicts as they arise.

LACK OF COMMITMENT

Filling out the middle tier of the dysfunction hierarchy is a **Lack of Commitment**. There's nothing worse than people who choose to be non-committal. Where there is no commitment, there is silence. And where there is silence, there is also violence. This is not the kind of violence that you're thinking of. It's not abuse or homicide, but rather a tumultuous unraveling of loyalty.

Indifference and apathy, which are side effects of disloyalty, brutally shake the foundations of a team in the absence of commitment.

In Revelation 3, we're given an example of a church that had waned in its commitment to Christ by falling in love with worldly things. In doing so, they developed an attitude of indifference. Because of their perpetual state of carelessness for godly things, God admonishes them. Similarly, when a team grows cold towards its purpose, the dedication of the individual team members begins to sputter. Revelation 3:16 goes on to say, "So, because you are lukewarm, and neither hot nor cold, I will spit you out of my mouth." Being lukewarm is the embodiment of no commitment. God states that people who can't commit to something experience relationship changes (Ex. spit you out of my mouth). Picture a man or woman being strung along with empty promises of marriage. Eventually, the waiting stops and people move on. While the book of Revelation gets into some pretty deep end-times imagery, we're just examining the principle of the above scripture. God wants our teams to be examples in the marketplace where we make confident and definitive decisions. Committed plans are established plans (Proverbs 16:3). Jesus said in Matthew 5:37, "Let what you say be simply 'Yes' or 'No'; anything more than this comes from evil."

Action: Pray and ask God how to deepen your commitment to him and your respective team.

AVOIDANCE OF ACCOUNTABILITY

The fourth stage of dysfunction in Lencioni's hierarchy is **Avoidance of Accountability**. When no one is accountable to anyone or anything, it bodes disaster. But we need to examine accountability from a slightly different perspective to understand why the lack of it is so crippling to a team. Accountability can be divided into two root words: account and ability. Account refers to someone giving an "account' for what action they were

supposed to take. This "giving of an account" is typically associated with "punishment" for not following through. Hence
phrases like "holding someone accountable." This statement, for
many, is grounded in fault rather than support because people
have the wrong view of accountability. But before someone can
give an account, they must first be given the "ability" to win.
They must be given ownership. Ownership refers to the tools
and resources needed for success. Once success factors have
been defined, then people are better equipped to be held
accountable. Consider the notion of doing what you say you're
going to do when you said you're going to do it. Then, ask
follow-up questions on why the goal wasn't met and what is
needed to hit the target next time.

This understanding of accountability sets up why the avoidance of it is so devastating. It means people are abdicating the
responsibility of taking ownership. It also means no one is being
questioned about follow-through. Patrick Lencioni describes the
Avoidance of Accountability this way, "Without committing to a
clear plan of action, even the most focused and driven people
often hesitate to call their peers on actions and behaviors that
seem counterproductive to the good of the team."[103]

Men and women have long struggled with accountability,
dating back to the Garden of Eden. God gave ownership of the
garden to the original team and first duo, Adam and Eve. They
were made in God's image and had perfect fellowship with Him,
lacking nothing. Adam and Eve, deceived by the serpent, ate
fruit from the Tree of Knowledge. Fear entered them for the
first time, and ashamed at what they had done, they hid themselves. When God questioned Adam about it, he blamed Eve.
Eve then blamed the serpent. Adam and Eve, though given
ownership of the garden, failed to give a proper account when
questioned.

The Bible contains within it many stories of God trying to
give man ownership, and man being unable to handle it. We
don't have to make the same mistake as Adam and Eve. Learn

from their missteps. As God-fearing teams, we must lean into God's Word to keep us accountable. It takes willingness and obedience (Isaiah 1:19).

Action: Pray and ask God to bring awareness to and removal of things in your life that keep you from being accountable.

INATTENTION TO RESULTS

The apex of the dysfunction pyramid is **Inattention To Results**. Lencioni says this transpires "when team members put their individual needs (such as ego, career development, or recognition) or even the needs of their divisions above the collective goals of the team."[104] By this point in the pyramid, all of the dysfunctions have had a compounding effect. When things fall apart, people look out for number one, themselves, even if it's at the detriment of other team members.

King David, the man after God's own heart, was guilty of putting his needs above the nation of Israel. Instead of leading his army into battle, he stayed behind at home. This lack of focus led him to partake in temptation. One day while overlooking the city from his tower, he saw a beautiful woman named Bathsheba bathing naked. He had his servant call her to his quarters, and he slept with her. One thing led to another, and David found himself in a scandal because she was married to one of his soldiers. He got Bathsheba pregnant, and worse, devised a plan to murder her husband to cover it up.

David was a Warrior King, and when his team needed him most, he wasn't there. His lustful passions outgrew leading his team to victory. When we are focused on the collective result rather than individual ones, we are better positioned to win. Learn from David's mistake and keep your eye on the group's greater task at hand.

Action: Pray and ask God to remove distractions out of your life, so you don't fall prey to team shattering temptations.

ADVERSITY BUILDS CHARACTER

To say that the 2020 Superbowl Champion Kansas City Chiefs had a magical season would be an understatement. But even their storybook ending didn't come without trials. In fact, the Chiefs learned how to thrive under extreme pressure. They became the first team in NFL history with three double-digit comeback wins in the same postseason.[105] One of their comebacks, in particular, a 51-31 win over the Houston Texans, was also the largest come from behind victory (a 24-point deficit) in franchise history.[106] In the Superbowl post-game interview, Kansas City Chiefs Chairman Clark Hunt put the successful season into perspective (paraphrased): "The journey is a big part of it... it wouldn't be what it is without the hardship, without all the hard work that went into getting us here."[107]

Part of God's growth process for us as believers is building our character in the midst of adversity. James 1:2-4 says, "Count it all joy, my brothers, when you meet trials of various kinds, for you know that the testing of your faith produces steadfastness. And let steadfastness have its full effect, that you may be perfect and complete, lacking in nothing." In this text, James is talking about how our faith in God gets tested during the trials of life and the resulting steadfastness that gets produced. We tend to go through growth processes as teams as well. When you persevere through business pressures like cash flow management, operating expenses, profit margins, and inventory, it refines you into a stronger, more enduring worker. Two different kinds of growth, but both moving along an axis of maturity. However, your growth at work doesn't have to be separate from God. He desires to know you in every way. If you grow in your intimacy with Christ, your renewed character will permeate into other areas of your life, such as business. Jesus has already overcome the world, and that includes the burdens of business. We just need to do our part by standing steadfast in what God has already done, what he's presently doing, and what he will do in the future.

FEEDBACK, FEEDBACK, FEEDBACK

In Disney's *Remember The Titans*, you may recall the infamous war of words between team star players Julius Campbell and Gerry Bertier. After a stretch of strenuous three-a-day practices, both players reached a breaking point and called each other out in this eye-opening scene:[108]

Bertier: Listen, I'm Gerry, you're Julius. Let's just get some particulars and get this over with.

Big Ju: Particulars? Man, no matter what I tell you, you ain't never gonna know nothing about me.

Bertier: Listen, I ain't running any more of these three-a-days

Big Ju: Well, what I've got to say, you really don't wanna hear 'cuz honesty ain't too high upon your people's priorities list.

Bertier: Honesty? You want honesty? Alright, honestly, I think you're nothing. Nothing but a pure waste of God-given talent. You don't listen to nobody, man! Not even Doc or Boone! Shiver push on the line every time, and you blow right past 'em! Push 'em, pull 'em, do something! You can't run over everybody in this league, and every time you do, you leave one of your teammates hanging out to dry, me in particular!

Big Ju: Why should I give a hoot about you, huh? Or anyone else out there? You wanna talk about the ways you're the captain, right?

Bertier: Right.

Big Ju: You got a job?

Bertier: I've got a job.

Big Ju: You been doing your job?

Bertier: I've been doing my job.

Big Ju: Then why don't you tell your white buddies to block for Rev better? Because they have not blocked for him worth a plug nickel, and you know it! Nobody plays. Yourself included. I'm supposed to wear myself out for the team? What team? Nah, nah what I'm gonna do is look out for myself and I'ma get mine.

Bertier: See man, that's the worst attitude I ever heard.

Big Ju: Attitude reflects leadership, captain.

Those were scathing exchanges between Bertier and Campbell, but it did cause them to look inward at themselves. Responding like great leaders, they accepted the feedback and applied it. Their honest assessments of each other helped fortify the team's chemistry and established a winning culture. A vital detail in this situation was the character of Gerry and Julius. They already had the team's respect. When receiving feedback, consider the source it's coming from.

The **Feedback Creates Accountability** model in *The Oz Principle* is a great resource to consider using for both giving and receiving feedback.

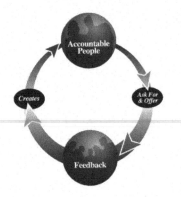

In the above diagram, authors Roger Connors, Tom Smith, and Craig Hickman give us a clear and understandable way to gain the most authentic feedback:[109]

 1. Ask for feedback in the right environment (a comfortable,

quiet place free from interruptions and distractions).

2. Tell the person from whom you're seeking feedback that you want completely honest input about a particular situation or concern. Emphasize your sincerity and explain your motivation.

3. Remember, the feedback you're requesting represents an important point of view, so don't get defensive, even if you strongly disagree with something the person says.

4. Listen carefully and ask for elaboration, but be sure not to invalidate feedback off-handedly with which you disagree.

No one understood feedback more clearly than our Lord and Savior, Jesus Christ. In Revelation 2, Jesus issues what appears to be a tough criticism of the seven churches. However, if you look closely, Jesus provides graceful recommendations for the churches to walk in their true calling. In these passages, we find that Jesus uses what's commonly known as the **"Feedback Sandwich."** The sandwich is made of three ingredients: a top bun of opening positive statements, a middle burger patty of improvement, and a bottom bun of reassurance. To better understand this pattern, observe the Letter to Ephesus in Revelation 2:1-7:

"To the angel of the church in Ephesus write: 'The words of him who holds the seven stars in his right hand, who walks among the seven golden lampstands.

Top Bun Opening Positive Statement {"'I know your works, your toil and your patient endurance, and how you cannot bear with those who are evil, but have tested those who call themselves apostles and are not, and found them to be false. I know you are enduring patiently and bearing up for my name's sake, and you have not grown weary.}

Middle Burger Patty Improvement {But I have this against you, that you have abandoned the love you had at first. Remember, therefore, from where you have fallen; repent, and do the works you did at first. If not, I will come to you and remove your lampstand from its place, unless you repent.}

Bottom Bun Assurance {Yet this you have: you hate the

works of the Nicolaitans, which I also hate. He who has an ear, let him hear what the Spirit says to the churches. To the one who conquers I will grant to eat of the tree of life, which is in the paradise of God.']

When we regularly give and receive feedback, it supplies us the ability to climb the highest of mountains and withstand the lowest of valleys in the marketplace.

BLIND SPOTS

They say adversity and crisis reveal who we are. Who we are under pressure exposes our blind spots. According to dictionary.com, a blind spot is "an area or subject about which one is uninformed, prejudiced, or unappreciative:"[110] Since we are totally unaware of blind spots, it's important to keep the right kinds of people around you. People who sharpen you. People who challenge you to be better. People who ask you to think outside of the box. The Bible gives three good examples of roles that can help identify blind spots in our life: an armor-bearer, a teacher, and a mentor.

Armor-bearer – By definition, an armor-bearer is an "... attendant bearing the armor or arms of a warrior or knight (partial)."[111] Armor-bearers are astute at seeing one's blind spots because they are detailed, have keen awareness, and are honorable.

1 Samuel 14:13 - **Detailed**

"Then Jonathan climbed up on his hands and feet, and his armor-bearer after him. And they fell before Jonathan, and his armor-bearer killed them after him."

While Jonathan started the attack, his armorbearer was thorough by finishing the attack, ensuring the enemy was totally eliminated. A detailed person helps you close loopholes.

2 Samuel 18:15 – **Keen Awareness**

"And ten young men, Joab's armor-bearers, surrounded Absalom and struck him and killed him."

Joab's armor-bearers knew the terrain and completely surrounded the enemy so there would be no escape. People with a systems-thinking view, have the alertness of mind to scout the environment.

1 Samuel 31:5 – **Honorable**

"And when his armor-bearer saw that Saul was dead, he also fell upon his sword and died with him."

Saul's armor-bearer lived only to serve Saul. He was honorable unto death. Honorable people are devoted, have high integrity, and will help you weed out foolishness.

Teacher – Teachers identify blind spots by enlightening us with new information, concepts, and insight previously unknown. They often teach us something new or deepen our knowledge of a known subject matter.

Acts 18:24-26

"Now a Jew named Apollos, a native of Alexandria, came to Ephesus. He was an **eloquent** man, **competent** in the Scriptures. He had been **instructed in the way** of the Lord. And being **fervent** in spirit, he **spoke and taught accurately** the things concerning Jesus, though he knew only the baptism of John. He began to **speak boldly** in the synagogue, but when Priscilla and Aquila heard him, they **took him aside** and explained to him the way of God more accurately."

The Bible shows us that this particular teacher, Apollos, was eloquent, competent, came from a good pedigree, spoke with passion, taught accurately, was a bold speaker, and was teachable. These kinds of teachers unlock our capacity to reach new levels of learning, thus closing the gap on our blind spots.

Mentor – Mentors point out blind spots with their sage advice based on life experiences.

Titus 1:4-5

"To Titus, my true child in a common faith: Grace and peace from God the Father and Christ Jesus our Savior. This is why I left you in Crete, so that you might put what remained into order, and appoint elders in every town **as I directed you—**"

We see from scripture that mentors (Paul, in this case) treat their mentees almost like sons and daughters. This comes with the expectation of the mentee not repeating the mistakes of the mentor and taking direction to heart. The close-knit kinship of a mentor creates honesty (different from a friendship) that addresses blind spots.

Thank God for rewarding relationships, else we would be flying blind. When we surround ourselves with wise counsel, it better prepares us to go into the storms of life and business. Seek the Lord and pray for an armor-bearer, a teacher, and a mentor. When you don't have these kinds of individuals in your life, you can exercise poor judgment. Poor judgment perpetuates ignorance of your blind spots. If you make poor judgment a habit, you'll fall apart during hard times.

CHAPTER TAKEAWAYS

1. There are consequences for failing to address the 5 Dysfunctions (Absence of Trust, Fear of Conflict, Lack of Commitment, Avoidance of Accountability, Inattention to Results).
2. Consider using the "Feedback Sandwich" (Top Positive Statement, Middle Improvement, Bottom Assurance).
3. Pray for and seek out an armor-bearer, a teacher, and a mentor.

REST WELL

"FOR IN SIX DAYS THE LORD MADE HEAVEN AND EARTH, THE SEA, AND ALL THAT IS IN THEM, AND RESTED ON THE SEVENTH DAY. THEREFORE, THE LORD BLESSED THE SABBATH DAY AND MADE IT HOLY."

— EXODUS 20:11

"THERE IS VIRTUE IN WORK, AND THERE IS VIRTUE IN REST. USE BOTH AND OVERLOOK NEITHER."

— ALAN COHEN

REST BRINGS REFRESHMENT

In Mark 2:27, Jesus reminds the Pharisees what the original intent of the Sabbath was after they questioned the disciples' plunking of grain. "And he said to them, 'The Sabbath was made for man, not man for the Sabbath.'" God set the example for rest back in the Garden of Eden. He set aside one day that had no work associated with it. God is all-powerful and doesn't require rest in the human sense. But he created a fulfilling type of rest for us, knowing man would have a tendency to work till extreme exhaustion. The principle of the Sabbath involves the intentional setting aside of time. Stress, anxiety, depression, and many other mental health conditions are at all-time highs in the workplace. Men and women concern themselves with the cares of this world, thus ignoring the benefits of what rest brings. One of the major advantages of rest is refreshment. Let's look at the word refresh a little closer. It's broken into two parts: the prefix "re" and the base "fresh." Re means "again." Fresh means "new." When we take time to rest, we become like "new again." In order to accomplish the purpose which God has called us to in the marketplace, we must be at our best by "accepting" the Sabbath time God set before us.

TIME AWAY

Many of us intend to take meaningful action on various occasions but find ourselves not doing so. Taking time off is one of the simplest actions we can take to rest and recover. Yet, people do not take off for a host of reasons. This behavior permeates the work culture. According to research done by the U.S. Travel Association, Oxford Economics, and Ipsos, 768 million U.S. vacation hours went unused in 2018.[112] 768 million! Looking deeper into the data, researchers found that 80% of workers said travel was important.[113] However, planning was the key element in workers who used more of their time off versus those who didn't plan.[114] Now travel isn't the only activity to do when taking off. You could visit a historical site, take up a physical activity (Ex. Sport, hiking), or maybe go on a retreat. The key is to be intentional by setting aside the time and then actually taking time off. Don't just decide, do.

Awareness is the catalyst that drives intentionality. We can look to the example of Jesus for always having a wise sense of knowing "when" to withdraw and step away.

John 6:15

"**Perceiving** then that they were about to come and take him by force to make him king, **Jesus withdrew** again to the mountain by himself."

Matthew 12:15

"**Jesus**, **aware** of this, **withdrew** from there. And many followed him, and he healed them all."

Matthew 14:13

"**Now when Jesus heard this**, he **withdrew** from there in a boat to a desolate place by himself. But when the crowds heard it, they followed him on foot from the towns."

Do you know how many days or weeks you can go without a break? Are you truly resting on the weekend? What is your current stress level? Does your company offer the right vacation policy needed to fit you and your family? These are the kinds of questions to consider thinking through. As a result of doing this kind of introspection, your area of awareness will expand.

REFLECTIVE THINKING

> "**The true currency of life is time, not money, and we've all got a limited stock of that.**"
>
> — **ROBERT HARRIS**

Time off and time away is of good profit. Doing so allows one to take inventory on what really matters. In John Maxwell's *How Successful People Think*, he walks us through the eleven ways accomplished people think. In chapter 7 of the book, John introduces us to **Reflective Thinking**. He metaphorically describes it as such: "being like the crock-pot of the mind. It encourages your thoughts to simmer until they're done."[115] Slowing down and taking your time allows you to experience the benefits of reflective thinking. John goes on to show us the five significant advantages of this thinking pattern:[116]

1. **Reflective Thinking gives you a true perspective.**
2. **Reflective Thinking gives emotional integrity to your thought life.**
3. **Reflective Thinking increases your confidence in decision making.**
4. **Reflective Thinking clarifies the big picture.**
5. **Reflective Thinking takes a good experience and makes it a valuable experience.**

The Bible encourages this kind of thoughtful reflection. God knows that the mind is the true battlefield. More wars are fought mentally long before they manifest into a physical confrontation. Scripture lovingly guides us down a path of restful thinking.

Psalm 46:10 – **Stillness is key**

"**Be still, and know** that I am God. I will be exalted among the nations. I will be exalted in the earth!"

Proverbs 23:7 KJV (partial) – **Identity Check**

"For as he **thinketh** in his **heart**, so **is** he..."[117]

Philippians 4:8 – **Meaningful Matters**

"Finally, brothers, whatever is true, whatever is honorable, whatever is just, whatever is pure, whatever is lovely, whatever is commendable, if there is any excellence, if there is anything worthy of praise, **think about these things**."

Romans 12:2 – **Spiritual Mind Renewal (From God's Word)**

"Do not be conformed to this world, but be transformed by the **renewal of your mind**, that by testing you may discern what is the will of God, what is good and acceptable and perfect."

Colossians 3:2 – **Christ Focus**

"**Set your minds on things** that are **above**, not on things that are on earth."

A time of rest creates space for reflection. A time for reflection sets the tone for renewal. Renewal kindles in us the reminder that we've been redeemed by the blood of the lamb! Get fired up upon your return to the workplace shouting the resounding praise from Psalm 107:2 "Let the redeemed of the Lord say so, whom he has redeemed from trouble."

REST BRINGS SUSTAINABILITY

Earlier in the chapter, we discussed how rest brings the benefit of refreshment. There's another primary benefit of rest. Rest also brings replenishment. To replenish means "to make full or complete again, as by supplying what is lacking, used up, etc.:"[118] Refreshment (being made new again) plus replenishment (being refilled) equals sustainability. Rest affects your ability to sustain your productivity. Sustained productivity over time creates a competitive advantage in business. We can learn from one solid example of sustainability in software development. There's a concept known as "husbandry." In order to maintain good quality products, companies need to complete activities like system upgrades and security patches. These tasks "keep the lights" to protect the viability of product operations.

Sadly, we tend to be forced into times of rest. Long hours at the office, day after day, take a toll on us. Working at this frenetic pace, two notable areas that begin to decline quickly are our mental and physical health. Our heavenly Father cares deeply about our well-being and showers us with comfort in his Word on these two affairs.

Psalm 55:22 – **Hardship, Stress, Anxiety (Mental Health)**

"Cast your **burden** on the Lord, and he will **sustain** you; he will never permit the righteous to be moved."

Psalm 41:3 (partial) – **Sickness (Physical Health)**

"The Lord **sustains** him on his **sickbed**..."

REPLENISHMENT

We already defined what replenishment is earlier, but there's more to it. We need to understand that replenishment is a principle in scripture, not just a one-time event. Romans 15:13 mentions how God "fills" us with joy and peace. Replenishment is a process of repetition that takes place while we are at rest. Think about how race cars enter pit road during a NASCAR race. It's not unusual to see cars get a new set of tires and refuel during a pit stop. Could you imagine trying to change the tires on a moving car? What about refueling? It would be a disaster! When we rest, we must allow ourselves to be filled up completely, so we're not lacking anything.

ENCOURAGEMENT

Perhaps the most powerful thing we can receive during a time of rest is encouragement. Encouragement is like jet fuel for the soul. Encouragement does, however, come at a cost. It comes at the cost of "seeking." The good news is when you are taking a Sabbath, you are positioned to seek. Pursuing encouragement is two-fold: finding someone else to encourage, then being encouraged yourself. Ironically, when you encourage someone else, you yourself get encouraged. There's a transformational flow of joy between people when encouragement is being distributed. What better way to return to the office than to have added value to someone else, and subsequently had value added to you yourself?

Why does encouragement have this seismic impact on us? The Bible gives us three profound explanations:

Romans 15:5 - **God is the God of encouragement**

"May the **God of** endurance and **encouragement** grant you to live in such harmony with one another, in accord with Christ Jesus."

Romans 15:4 - **Encouragement brings hope**

"For whatever was written in former days was written for our instruction, that through endurance and through the **encouragement** of the Scriptures **we might have hope**."

Hebrews 3:13 AMP - **Encouragement shields us from the deception of sin**

"But continually **encourage** one another every day, as long as it is called "Today" [and there is an opportunity], **so that none of you will be hardened** [into settled rebellion] by the **deceitfulness of sin** [its cleverness, delusive glamour, and sophistication]."[119]

Encouragement isn't a man-made potion of passion. It's a divine medicine that brings rest and healing to the heart.

CHAPTER TAKEAWAYS

1. God created the Sabbath (time of rest) for man.
2. Rest brings refreshment.
3. Rest brings replenishment.

SPIRIT OF CONTINUOUS IMPROVEMENT

"AND JESUS INCREASED IN WISDOM AND IN STATURE AND IN FAVOR WITH GOD AND MAN."

— LUKE 2:52

"GOOD, BETTER, BEST. NEVER LET IT REST. TIL YOUR GOOD IS BETTER AND YOUR BETTER IS BEST."

— ST. JEROME

LEARNING IS THE BRIDGE TO IMPROVEMENT

This book has been a graceful marathon about being planted in God's way of business and work. As we come around the bend for the final lap, let us take time to understand the value of having a growth mindset. God the Father gave us his finest when he sent his son Jesus to die on the cross for our sins. He also gave us a sixty-six-book love letter to counsel every aspect of our life, including business. Not out of striving or owing, we should give him our best to emulate his example of giving "the best." God is love, and His love is perfect. Because his perfect love showers us daily, we can draw the strength to be excellent in the work we do. The way we steward our excellence is through continuous learning. Continuous learning, once established, leads to continuous improvement. The Japanese have a term for this called "kaizen (continuous improvement)." This process begins with a personal growth plan. We must grow first before we ask others to improve.

John Maxwell lays out an exceptional playbook for developing a growth plan in his book *The 15 Invaluable Law of Growth*. Though all of the laws are profound in their own way, I quickly want to touch on three of the laws that really stand out to me. I will also pair them with Bible verses that reinforce the message.

The Law of Intentionality – Growth doesn't just happen

Ultimately, nobody is responsible for your growth but you. Many of us make the gross assumption that someone else is supposed to look out for us. John Maxwell says, "It's the growing through life that sets you apart from those who are just going through life."[120]

Ephesians 5:15-17

"**Look carefully then how you walk**, not as unwise but as wise, making the best use of the time, because the days are evil. Therefore, do not be foolish, but understand what the will of the Lord is."

The Law of Awareness – Know yourself to grow yourself

Growth moves at the speed of self-awareness. To not be self-aware is to be a pilot flying blind.[121]

Psalm 26:2

"Prove me, O LORD, and try me; **test my heart and my mind.**"

The Law of Consistency – Consistency keeps you growing

Consistency is the sum of motivation and discipline. Motivation is a great starter, but discipline is the great sustainer.[122]

1 Corinthians 15:58

"Therefore, my beloved brothers, **be steadfast, immov-**

able, always abounding in the work of the Lord, knowing that in the Lord your labor is not in vain."

EQUIPPING

Once we've established our own personal growth plan, we can now look to train and develop others. My lovely wife and Business Strategist, Desola Davis, gives a wonderful list of five must-haves that equip people and businesses for doing the next right thing.[123]

1. **Vision** – Why you do something determines what you do.
2. **Plan** – If you fail to plan, plan to fail. Determine when you need to persevere forward with the plan or pivot to a new strategy.
3. **System** – Implement an efficient system to consistently deliver value to the customer. Reduce wasteful activities that don't add value.
4. **Accountability** – Don't wait for someone to ask. Have the courage to **see it.** Find the heart to **own it.** Obtain the wisdom to **solve it.** Exercise the means to **do it.**[124]
5. **Kaizen** – If you don't intentionally get better, you are unintentionally getting worse.

When you identify and do the "next right thing," you better position yourself to exponentially achieve business outcomes. In the same way, seek the Lord for strategic direction, and he will guide your decisions and administration.

HABITS

"We are what we repeatedly do. Excellence, therefore, is not an act, but a habit."

— ARISTOTLE

Equipping readies us for learning and improvement. Habits mold our learning into actionable behaviors. What we do or don't do on a daily basis is what determines our success. Our personal habits, no doubt, bleed into our professions. Because of the interconnected nature of how life works, we must be intentional with and stay motivated by pursuing good habits. In his book, *Better Than Good*, Zig Ziglar encourages us to cultivate eleven indispensable habits. If you know anything about Zig Ziglar, you don't have to guess where he learned these from. That's right. The B-I-B-L-E!

The Habit of Staying Motivated (1)[125] – Zig put it best: "When you make motivation a habit, you will get wherever it is you want to go more quickly and have considerably more fun on the trip." Do you have the right motivation?

Colossians 3:23 – "Whatever you do, work heartily, as for the Lord and not for men,"

The Habit of Listening (2)[126] – Listen to understand. Don't just prepare your next response. It's a sign of respect, and you'll probably learn something you never knew.

James 1:19 – "Know this, my beloved brothers: let every person be quick to hear, slow to speak, slow to anger;"

The Habit of Learning (3)[127] – Radical growth comes from habitual learning.

Proverbs 18:15 – "An intelligent heart acquires knowledge, and the ear of the wise seeks knowledge."

The Habit of Reading (4)[128] – "The person who doesn't read is no better off than the person who can't read." – Zig Ziglar

And what we read matters.

Joshua 1:8 – "This Book of the Law shall not depart from your mouth, but you shall meditate on it day and night, so that you may be careful to do according to all that is written in it. For then you will make your way prosperous, and then you will have good success."

The Habit of Redeeming the Time (5)[129] – Use your time wisely, especially during the daily commute. Listen to a podcast. Use services like Audible or Scribd to listen to audiobooks. Turn your car into a school on wheels.

Psalm 90:12 – "So teach us to number our days that we may get a heart of wisdom."

The Habit of Doing Your Best (6)[130] – "Never settle for anything less than your best." – Brian Tracy

When you give your best, people tend to notice. Giving your best has more to do with the condition of your soul.

Proverbs 13:4 – "The soul of the sluggard craves and gets nothing, while the soul of the diligent is richly supplied."

The Habit of Health (7)[131] – Your body is a temple. Care for it in every way (spiritually, physically, mentally, emotionally).

1 Corinthians 6:19-20 – "Or do you not know that your body is a temple of the Holy Spirit within you, whom you have from God? You are not your own, for you were bought with a price. So glorify God in your body."

The Habit of Rest (8)[132] – Prioritize going to sleep. Fall asleep to peaceful music. Wear a mask to block out the light. Get earplugs to block out sound.

Psalm 127:2 – "It is in vain that you rise up early and go late to rest, eating the bread of anxious toil; for he gives to his beloved sleep."

The Habit of Self-Discipline (9)[133] – Discipline = Responsible + Reliable

2 Timothy 1:7 – "for God gave us a spirit not of fear but of power and love and self-control."

The Habit of Going the Extra Mile (10)[134] – Having a servant's heart results in opportunism and advancement.

Philippians 2:3-4 – "Do nothing from selfish ambition or conceit, but in humility count others more significant than yourselves. Let each of you look not only to his own interests but also to the interests of others."

The Habit of Pure Thoughts (11)[135] – "...fill your mind with positive and moral thoughts." – Zig Ziglar Good inputs lead to good outputs. Immoral inputs lead to immoral outputs.

Romans 8:5-6 – "For those who live according to the flesh set their minds on the things of the flesh, but those who live according to the Spirit set their minds on the things of the Spirit. For to set the mind on the flesh is death, but to set the mind on the Spirit is life and peace."

Ziglar's eleven power habits are gems in their own right. But to properly use them to your advantage, you must understand how habits work. In James Clear's *Atomic Habits*, he breaks down the four-step pattern that makes up every habit called the "Habit Loop." The four parts of the Habit Loop include a **Cue, Craving, Response, and Reward**.[136] To explain the stages, I'll use someone sending a text to your phone as an example. The cue would be the sound of a text notification. The alert then elicits in you a desire to check the text (craving). Your response is the physical lifting of the phone to check the text message. The reward is the satisfaction you get out of knowing both the sender of the text and the subject matter of the text.

Similarly, God cues us with his voice, circumstantial events, and through other people. Our craving comes from a desire to be obedient to his voice. This, in turn, creates a response of thanksgiving. The reward is God doing more than we could ever ask or imagine (Ephesians 3:20 NLT).[137]

BUILDING A LEARNING ORGANIZATION

"As the world becomes more interconnected and business becomes more complex and dynamic, work must become more "learningful."

— PETER M. SENGE

At every corner of the world, business problems become more and more sophisticated. There's no way a single subject matter expert like a founder, CEO, or talented board member can solve economic challenges on their own. Problems must be solved another way. In Disney's *Avengers: Age of Ultron*, when asked how to defeat the insurmountable enemy, Captain America provided a matter-of-fact answer: "Together."[138] Rolling up your sleeves and attacking obstacles as a team is the way forward. In his book *The Fifth Discipline: The Art and Practice of The Learning Organization*, Peter M. Senge proposes that "learning" together is the way to deal with business problems. Senge goes on to explain how real organizational improvement occurs through five disciplines. You'll find that these disciplines have Biblical roots.

PERSONAL MASTERY

Great companies consist of great people. And people are great at what they do, because of being personally invested in the mastery of learning. Peter Senge defines personal mastery this way: "Personal mastery is the discipline of continually clarifying and deepening our personal vision, of focusing our energies, of developing patience, and of seeing reality objectively."[139] We can identify instances of learning and development in scripture.

Proverbs 1:5 – "Let the wise hear and increase in learning, and the one who understands obtain guidance,"

Proverbs 9:9 – "Give instruction to a wise man, and he will be still wiser; teach a righteous man, and he will increase in learning."

MENTAL MODELS

Mental models "determine not only how we make sense of the world, but how we take action."[140] Mental models heavily influence company culture. In *The Lean Startup*, Eric Ries champions rigorous use of the Scientific method for product development. Applying the Scientific Method, as a mental model for value creation, suggests that a company favors the approach of rapid experimentation for pursuing profitable outcomes. Another example of a mental model is the use of Agile practices within software development. The Agile Manifesto (in its purest form), a set of four values and twelve principles, acts as a guide for creating working software. We can list hundreds of mental models, but the bottom line is which ones are relevant and spur growth. James Clear states that "the best mental models are the ideas with the most utility. They are broadly useful in daily life."[141] The Bible flips many business mental models on their head because God's ways are far above man's ways (Isaiah 55:8-9).

Man's way: Judge By The Outer Appearance

God's way: 1 Samuel 16: 7 – "But the Lord said to Samuel, "Do not look on his appearance or on the height of his stature, because I have rejected him. For the Lord sees not as man sees: man looks on the outward appearance, but **the Lord looks on the heart**."

Man's way: Money (Profit) Matters Most

God's way: Matthew 6:24 – "No one can serve two masters, for either he will hate the one and love the other, or he will be devoted to the one and despise the other. **You cannot serve God and money**."

Man's way: Lead With Aggression And Dominance

God's way: John 13:14 – "If I then, your Lord and Teacher, have washed your feet, you also ought to **wash one another's feet**."

Matthew 20:28 – "even as the Son of Man **came not to be served but to serve**, and to give his life as a ransom for many."

BUILDING SHARED VISION

There is no greater call to action in business than setting a vision. Vision has a ripple effect. Certain pockets of an organization can catch the vision, but the real power takes place when an entire organization embraces the vision collectively. Senge frames the effect of vision this way: "Personal visions derive their power from an individual's deep caring for the vision. Shared visions derive their power from a common caring."[142] The shared sense of cherishing a company's purpose incites a desire to learn and aim to be better.

The early Church in the Book of Acts carried a collective bond. In fact, they held "all things in common (Acts 2:44)." The love of Christ operated in them deeply because they were committed in four specific areas:

1. The Apostles' teaching
2. Fellowship
3. Breaking of bread
4. Prayers

Acts 2:42

"And they devoted themselves to the **apostles' teaching** and the **fellowship**, to the **breaking of bread** and the **prayers**."

Building a shared vision God's way creates clarity and momentum. Clarity and momentum to do what? Let our light (Jesus) shine before men while enhancing society with our gifts and talents (good works).

TEAM LEARNING STARTS WITH DIALOGUE

You've heard it said before that communication is key. Communication drives the quality of relationships. What may not be top of mind is how communication springboards teams down a path of learning. To communicate effectively is to be aligned by like-minded dialogue. Four areas of dialogue (based on my personal experience) that are essential to a team's learning are a dialogue of purpose, a dialogue of personality, a dialogue of function, and a dialogue of vocabulary.

Dialogue of purpose – Teams must understand why they exist and how they serve the greater organization.

Dialogue of personality – The better that teams get to know each individual's disposition, the better they'll be able to work through conflict.

Dialogue of function – When teams know their general skillset(s), they can better operate in their strength zone and identify opportunities for improvement.

Dialogue of vocabulary – Teams must norm on the use of terminology to maintain clarity and avoid confusion.

Similarly, to Senge's point about starting team dialogue, the Bible tells us that Jesus began a team dialogue by creating a culture of learning based on two words: "Follow me."

Matthew 4:19 says, "And he said to them, "**Follow me**, and I will make you fishers of men."

Jesus appointed twelve men and called them "disciples." A disciple, by definition, is a follower. The followership of Christ, by way of the Holy Spirit, inspired the founding of the Church. The like-minded nature of the Church is to function as the "Body of Christ." When the underlying dialogue of your business is being Christ-like, you are following in his footsteps.

SYSTEMS THINKING

There is more at play than the individual tasks you complete on the job. What you do on a day to day basis is part of a larger structure. When you take a tunnel vision perspective of your job, you have what is known as localized thinking. This is very much in line with an industrial age mindset that focused on specialization and efficiency. Modern-day, we function in an information age, with an emphasis on collaboration. Information gets produced at greater rates than can be consumed. To combat this, a different kind of viewpoint is required, one that looks at the whole rather than the parts. This is systems thinking. Peter Senge defines his fifth and final organizational discipline, systems thinking, as "a framework for seeing interrelationships rather than things, for seeing patterns of change rather than static "snapshots."[143] Researchers Anne Murray Allen and Dennis Sandow described four shifts that took place in the transition from the industrial age to the knowledge age:[144]

1. Focusing on **parts to** focusing on the **whole**
2. Focusing on **categorization to** focusing on **integration**
3. Focusing on **individuals to** focusing on **interactions**
4. Focusing on **systems outside the observer to** focusing on **systems that include the observer**

The ability for man to see things as a whole comes from Jesus Christ. He is the ultimate seer because he is the Alpha and the Omega, the beginning and the end (Revelation 22:13). Jesus taught with incomprehensible wisdom, and through his teaching, the Bible informs us just how much of a systems thinker he happened to be. We can see instances of the four shifts discussed above in examining the life of Christ.

Focus on the whole

1 Corinthians 12:12 – "For just as the body is one and has many members, and all the members of the body, though many, are **one body**, so it is with Christ."

Focus on integration

John 17:21 – "that they **may all be one**, just as you, Father, are in me, and I in you, that they also may be in us, so that the world may believe that you have sent me."

Focus on interactions

John 13:34-35 – "A new commandment I give to you, that you **love one another**: just as I have loved you, you also are to love one another. By this all people will know that you are my disciples, if you have love for one another."

Focus on inclusion

Mark 2:17 – "And when Jesus heard it, he said to them, "Those who are well have no need of a physician, but those who are sick. **I came not to call the righteous, but sinners**."

When you become a systems thinker, you uncover the full blueprint to steward your business or role with eyes of understanding.

FINAL CHAPTER TAKEAWAYS

1. Improvement starts with you. Develop a personal growth plan.
2. Cultivate good habits.
3. Create a culture of learning within your organization.

PUTTING IT ALL TOGETHER

There is nothing that man has built, produced, or thought of that is his own. All innovation, ingenuity, creativity, and commerce come from Heaven above. Ecclesiastes 1:9-10 NLT says, "History merely repeats itself. It has all been done before. Nothing under the sun is truly new. Sometimes people say, "Here is something new!" But actually, it is old; nothing is ever truly new."[145] May we never grow arrogant or self-reliant in our economic pursuits, but rather be led by the Holy Spirit to serve the community around us.

Running a business, or working in and for a business, takes a lot of hard work. It also takes a great deal of faith. Faith that you'll get out of the bed in the morning. Faith that God will provide your needs. Faith to make shrewd business decisions. Faith that a group of people can accomplish a common set of goals. As believers called to the marketplace, we must "...never graduate from the University of Faith that teaches us to grow closer to God and closer to our own promised land."[146] This life can make your faith or take your faith. So, will you conform to the world's way of doing business, or will you transform by doing business God's way?

Manage well.

THE END

DECLARATIONS

God desires us to seek him in all that we do. I want to leave you with some declarations of blessing upon your family, business, employees, roles, and positions.

A Closer Relationship With God

I pray that you grow in your intimacy with God, that you learn more about his character by reading his Word, and that you seek him in all that you do. In the name of Jesus.

"Jabez was more honorable than his brothers; and his mother called his name Jabez, saying, "Because I bore him in pain." Jabez called upon the God of Israel, saying, "Oh that you would bless me and enlarge my border, and that your hand might be with me, and that you would keep me from harm so that it might not bring me pain!" And God granted what he asked."

— 1 CHRONICLES 4:9-10 – THE PRAYER OF
JABEZ

You shall be more honorable than your competition and co-workers. I pray that the Lord blesses you, that he enlarges your border (love of God, boldness for evangelism, influence, generosity), that his hand be with you (favor), and that he keeps you from harm and pain (politics, lay-offs, and the like). In the name of Jesus.

SUCCESS

Everything discussed in this book would be for naught if you don't remember where your opportunity to succeed comes from. Success in the workplace comes from two places:

(1) Seeking God - Matthew 6:33

"But seek first the kingdom of God and his righteousness, and all these things will be added to you."

What are "these things?"

Matthew 6:25

"Therefore I tell you, do not be anxious about your life, **what you will eat** or **what you will drink**, nor about your body, **what you will put on.** Is not life more than food, and the body more than clothing?"

(2) Willingness and Obedience To God - Isaiah 1:19

"If you are willing and obedient, you shall eat the good of the land;"

Go forth. Work and conduct business in the name of Jesus!

A CALL FOR SALVATION

Everything we've been talking about in this book is spiritual in nature. What God desires for his people to do and be at work.

These things come from having a personal relationship with God. One based on love. Not effort. Not striving. Whatever your background. No matter what you've been through, he desires to know you. He'll take your pain away. I know what he's done for me. He's delivered me from fear. He's held me up when I'm weak. He's my firm foundation when everything around me is falling apart. He gives me peace that passes human understanding. And he loves me unconditionally. God sent his Son, Jesus, to die on the cross for my sins. I needed a savior, and Jesus rescued me.

John 3:16

"For God so loved the world, that he gave his only Son, that whoever believes in him should not perish but have eternal life."

If you've never accepted Jesus Christ as your Lord and Savior, I'd like to extend you an invitation to know Jesus for yourself. His request is simple and two-fold: **confess** with your mouth that Jesus is Lord and **believe** in your heart that God raised him from the dead, and you will be saved.

Romans 10:9

"because, if you **confess with your mouth** that Jesus is Lord and **believe in your heart** that God raised him from the dead, you will be saved."

Pray this simple prayer right where you are:

Father, in the name of Jesus, I desire to be made new. I acknowledge my sin before you. I commit my life to you now by confessing with my mouth and believing in my heart that you died on the cross and rose again so that I might be saved. Thank you, Lord, for this gift of salvation. I now live as your son/daughter. Amen!

Congratulations! We're now united together in Christ! Heaven is rejoicing over you right now!

Luke 15:7

"Just so, I tell you, there will be more **joy in heaven over one sinner who repents** than over ninety-nine righteous persons who need no repentance."

Email us at info@jerichoforce.com so we can celebrate with you, connect with you, and help you join a good local church.

NOTES

[1]Pearcy, Nancy. Total Truth: Liberating Christianity from Its Cultural Captivity. February 15, 2008

[2]https://www.dictionary.com/browse/fruitful?s=t

[3]https://www.dictionary.com/browse/multiply?s=t

[4]Grudem, Wayne. Business For The Glory of God; The Bible's Teaching On The Moral Goodness of Business. 2003

[5]https://www.dictionary.com/browse/steward?s=t

[6]Maxwell, John C. Leadership 101. September 8, 2002

[7]Hunter, James C. The Servant: A Simple Story About the True Essence of Leadership. pg.27. June 10, 2008

[8]Scripture quotations marked NLT are taken from the *Holy Bible*, New Living Translation, copyright 1996, 2004, 2007, 2015 by Tyndale House Foundation. Used by permission of Tyndale House Publishers, Inc., Carol Stream, Illinois 60188. All rights reserved.

[9]Willink, Jocko. Discipline Equal Freedom Field Manual. October 17, 2007

[10]Maxwell, John C.. The 15 Invaluable Laws of Growth. October 2, 2012

[11]Lapin, Daniel. Thou Shall Prosper Second Edition: Ten Commandments For Making Money. October 2, 2009

[12]Doyle, Alison. What is the Average Hours Per Week Worked in the US?. July 3, 2019

[13]Jones, Jeffrey M.. U.S. Church Membership Down Sharply in Past Two Decades. April 18, 2009

[14]Spada, Doug. Scott, Dave. Monday Morning Atheist: Why We Switch God Off at Work and How You Fit It. pg.26. October 2, 2012

[15]The *Amplified* Bible is a Literal Equivalent translation that, by using synonyms and definitions, both explains and expands the meaning of words in the text by placing amplification in parentheses, brackets, and after keywords. This unique system of translation allows the reader to more completely and clearly grasp the meaning as it was understood in the original languages. Additionally, amplifications may provide further theological, historical, and other details for a better understanding of the text. Publisher: The Lockman Foundation

[16]Stevens, R. Paul. Work Matters: Lessons From Scripture. May 10, 2012

[17]Pope, Randy. Perimeter Church. Johns Creek, GA

[18]Blue, Ron. Moneywise Podcast

[19]Rainer, Art, The Money Challenge: 30 Days of Discovering God's Design for You and Your Money, May 5, 2017

[20]Bradly, Jayson D.. Church Giving Statistics, 2019 Edition. July 18, 2018

[21]Board of Governors of The Federal Reserve System. Report on the Economic Well-Being of U.S. Households in 2017. May 2018

[22]Krome, Charles. Car Depreciation: How Much Value Will a New Car Lose?. November 9, 2018

[23]Glover, Lacie. What You Can (And Can't) Learn From The Average Car Payment. December 21, 2018

[24]Investopedia Staff. 6 Reasons to Avoid Private Mortgage Insurance. January 15, 2020

[25]Scripture quotations marked NLT are taken from the *Holy Bible*, New Living Translation, copyright 1996, 2004, 2007, 2015

by Tyndale House Foundation. Used by permission of Tyndale House Publishers, Inc., Carol Stream, Illinois 60188. All rights reserved.

[26]Ramsey, Dave. The Total Money Makeover: A Proven Plan for Financial Fitness. September 17, 2013

[27]Jenkins, Lee. Lee Jenkins on Money: Real Solutions to Financial Challenges. September 23, 2009

[28]NEW AMERICAN STANDARD BIBLE® Copyright © 1960, 1962, 1963, 1968, 1971, 1972, 1973, 1975, 1977, 1995 by THE LOCKMAN FOUNDATION, A Corporation Not for Profit, LA HABRA, CA, All Rights Reserved, http://www.lockman.org

[29]Akindoju, Kunle. King's Court Chapel. Roswell, GA

[30]Kossman, Sienna. Poll: 4 in 10 co-signers lose money. June 6, 2016

[31]Scripture quotations marked NLT are taken from the *Holy Bible*, New Living Translation, copyright 1996, 2004, 2007, 2015 by Tyndale House Foundation. Used by permission of Tyndale House Publishers, Inc., Carol Stream, Illinois 60188. All rights reserved.

[32]Hogan, Chris. Live2Lead 2019. 12Stone Church. Lawrenceville, GA

[33]Greenleaf, Robert K.. The Servant As Leader. 1970

[34]Blanchard, Ken (April 8, 2015). Satisfaction & Great Results Come With Servant Leadership [https://www.youtube.com/watch?v=PDEgqbg40SM]. Retrieved from https://www.youtube.com/watch?v=PDEgqbg40SM

[35]Sinek, Simon (September 2009). How great leaders inspire action [https://www.youtube.com/watch?v=IPYeCltXpxw]. Retrieved from https://www.ted.com/talks/simon_sinek_how_great_leaders_inspire_action

[36]Sinek, Simon (September 2009). How great leaders inspire action [https://www.youtube.com/watch?v=IPYeCltXpxw]. Retrieved from https://www.ted.com/talks/simon_sinek_how_great_leaders_inspire_action

[37]The *Amplified* Bible is a Literal Equivalent translation that, by using synonyms and definitions, both explains and expands the meaning of words in the text by placing amplification in parentheses, brackets, and after keywords. This unique system of translation allows the reader to more completely and clearly grasp the meaning as it was understood in the original languages. Additionally, amplifications may provide further theological, historical, and other details for a better understanding of the text. Publisher: The Lockman Foundation

[38]Maxwell, John C.. The 21 Indispensable Qualities of a Leader: Becoming the Person Others Will Want to Follow. September 16, 2007

[39]https://www.dictionary.com/browse/followership?s=ts

[40]Warren, Rick. The Purpose Driven Life. pg.233. October 23, 2012

[41]Mansfield, Stephen. Ten Signs of a Leadership Crash. April 9, 2018

[42]Wiseman, Liz. Multipliers: How the Best Leaders Make Everyone Smarter. pg.20-23. June 15, 2010

[43]Schein, Edgar H.. Schein, Peter A.. Humble Leadership: The Power of Relationships, Openness, and Trust

[44]Schein, Edgar H.. Schein, Peter A.. Humble Leadership: The Power of Relationships, Openness, and Trust

[45]Davis Paul, Lea. Truett Cathy. Nontraditional All The Way. November/December 1997

[46]The *Amplified* Bible is a Literal Equivalent translation that, by using synonyms and definitions, both explains and expands the meaning of words in the text by placing amplification in parentheses, brackets, and after keywords. This unique system of translation allows the reader to more completely and clearly grasp the meaning as it was understood in the original languages. Additionally, amplifications may provide further theological, historical, and other details for a better understanding of the text. Publisher: The Lockman Foundation

[47]Scripture quotations marked NLT are taken from the *Holy Bible*, New Living Translation, copyright 1996, 2004, 2007, 2015 by Tyndale House Foundation. Used by permission of Tyndale House Publishers, Inc., Carol Stream, Illinois 60188. All rights reserved.

[48]https://www.dictionary.com/browse/barometer?s=t

[49]Story, Mack. Defining Influence: Increasing Your Influence Increases Your Options. September 9, 2016

[50]Covey, Stephen M.R.. The Speed of Trust: The One Thing that Changes Everything. October 17, 2006

[51]https://www.imdb.com/title/tt2193021/quotes?ref_=tt_ql_trv_4

[52]The Balancing Act (April 23, 2018). Diamonds 101: How They Form and How They're Found [https://www.youtube.com/watch?v=vaNZ-8q5w60]. Retrieved from https://www.youtube.com/watch?v=vaNZ-8q5w60

[53]Scripture quotations marked NLT are taken from the *Holy Bible*, New Living Translation, copyright 1996, 2004, 2007, 2015 by Tyndale House Foundation. Used by permission of Tyndale House Publishers, Inc., Carol Stream, Illinois 60188. All rights reserved.

[54]https://www.dictionary.com/browse/ethics?s=t

[55]Dwyer-Owens, Dina. Values, Inc.: How Incorporating Values into Business and Life Can Change the World. March 1, 2015

[56]https://www.dictionary.com/browse/diligence#

[57]https://www.blueletterbible.org/lang/lexicon/lexicon.cfm?Strongs=H4195&t=ESV

[58]Dayton, Howard. Your Money Counts: The Biblical Guide to Earning, Spending, Saving, Investing, Giving, and Getting Out of Debt. April 25, 2011

[59]Blue, Ron. Never Enough?: 3 Keys to Financial Contentment. April 1, 2017

[60]https://www.blueletterbible.org/lang/lexicon/lexicon.cfm?Strongs=H2450&t=ESV

[61]Goldratt, Eliyahu M.. The Goal: A Business Graphic Novel. August 8, 2017

[62]https://www.dictionary.com/browse/strategy?s=t

[63]McChesney, Chris. The 4 Disciplines of Execution: Achieving Your Wildly Important Goals. April 24, 2012

[64]https://my.bible.com/reading-plans/13439-leadership-lessons-from-nehemiah

[65]https://my.bible.com/reading-plans/13439-leadership-lessons-from-nehemiah

[66]Liker, Jeffrey. The Toyota Way: 14 Management Principles from the World's Greatest Manufacturer. August 8, 2017

[67]Ramsey, Dave. The Dave Ramsey Show Podcast

[68]Jenkins, Ryan. How This Company Had Achieved the Lowest Employee Turnover Rate. February 25, 2009

[69]Tardy, Daniel. The Entrepreneur's Guide To Hiring. https://cdn.ramseysolutions.net/media/hope/entre/pdf/12_steps_to_a_good_hire.pdf

[70]© 1982 by Thomas Nelson, Inc. All rights reserved. Used by permission.

[71]Scripture quotations marked NLT are taken from the *Holy Bible*, New Living Translation, copyright 1996, 2004, 2007, 2015 by Tyndale House Foundation. Used by permission of Tyndale House Publishers, Inc., Carol Stream, Illinois 60188. All rights reserved.

[72]Lencioni, Patrick. Allan Mulally and Accountability. https://www.tablegroup.com/hub/post/alan-mulally/
. April 2017

[73]Ikonne, Ebenezer (June 13, 2018). Why Joy? [https://www.youtube.com/watch?v=Or3GhKsMBiY
Retrieved from https://www.youtube.com/watch?v=Or3GhKsMBiY

[74]Chapman, Gary, White, Paul. The 5 Languages of Appreciation in the Workplace: Empowering Organizations by Encouraging People. January 1, 2019

[75]Chapman, Gary, White, Paul. The 5 Languages of Appreci-

ation in the Workplace: Empowering Organizations by Encouraging People. January 1, 2019

[76]Chapman, Gary, White, Paul. The 5 Languages of Appreciation in the Workplace: Empowering Organizations by Encouraging People. January 1, 2019

[77]https://www.appreciationatwork.com/5-languages-appreciation-workplace-improve-employee-engagement/

[78]Ramsey, Dave. The Dave Ramsey Show. https://www.daveramsey.com/askdave/business-and-leadership/no-gossip-allowed)

[79]https://www.latimes.com/business/story/2020-01-27/wells-fargo-scandal

[80]https://www.latimes.com/business/story/2020-01-27/wells-fargo-scandal

[81]Holocracy.org. Why Practice Holocracy?. https://www.holacracy.org/explore/why-practice-holacracy

[82]Maxwell, John C.

[83]@StephenCurry30 (Stephen Curry). "Believer. Husband to @ayeshacurry
, father to Riley, Ryan and Canon, son, brother. Golden State Warriors guard. Davidson Wildcat. Philippians 4:13 #IWILL
" Twitter, https://twitter.com/StephenCurry30?ref_src= twsrc%5Egoogle%7Ctwcamp%5Eserp%7Ctwgr%5Eauthor

[84]Elizabeth, Lindsay. Steph Curry Explains Moment He Truly Became a Christian and 'Gave My Life To Christ'. June 9, 2019

[85]https://www.entreleadership.com/blog/podcasts/patrick-lencioni-ideal-team-player

[86]Lencioni, Patrick. The Ideal Team Player: How to Recognize and Cultivate The Three Essential Virtues. April 25, 2016

[87]Lencioni, Patrick. The Ideal Team Player: How to Recognize and Cultivate The Three Essential Virtues. April 25, 2016

[88]Lencioni, Patrick. The Ideal Team Player: How to Recognize and Cultivate The Three Essential Virtues. April 25, 2016

[89]https://www.blueletterbible.org/search/search.cfm?Criteria= humble&t=ESV#s=s_primary_0_1

[90]Lencioni, Patrick. The Ideal Team Player: How to Recognize and Cultivate The Three Essential Virtues. April 25, 2016

[91]Hidden, Jeff. Victory Church. Acworth, Georgia

[92]Newton, Sonny. Souly Business - Talk 7: Finishing Well. January 26, 2020

[93]https://www.imdb.com/title/tt0094291/quotes?ref_=tt_ql_trv_4

[94]Lencioni, Patrick. The Ideal Team Player: How to Recognize and Cultivate The Three Essential Virtues. April 25, 2016

[95]Harvard Business Review. HBR's 10 Must Reads on Emotional Intelligence (with featured article "What Makes a Leader?" by Daniel Goleman). pg.6. April 7, 2015

[96]Harvard Business Review. HBR's 10 Must Reads on Emotional Intelligence (with featured article "What Makes a Leader?" by Daniel Goleman). pg.6. April 7, 2015

[97]Maxwell, John C.. The 17 Indisputable Laws of Teamwork: Embrace Them and Empower Your Team. April 1, 2013

[98]© Bruce Tuckman 1965 original 'Forming-storming-norming-performing' concept; Alan Chapman 2001-2013 review and code.

[99]Hackman, J. Richard. Leading Effective Teams: Setting the Stage for Great Performances. pg.40-41. July 10, 2002

[100]Hackman, J. Richard. Leading Effective Teams: Setting the Stage for Great Performances. July 10, 2002

[101]Covey, Stephen M.R.. The Speed of Trust: The One Thing that Changes Everything. October 17, 2006

[102]https://www.webmd.com/diabetes/qa/what-is-gangrene

[103]Lencioni, Patrick. The Five Dysfunctions of a Team: A Leadership Fable. November 17, 2011

[104]Lencioni, Patrick. The Five Dysfunctions of a Team: A Leadership Fable. November 17, 2011

[105]Stephen, Eric. The Chiefs set an NFL record with their Super Bowl comeback. February 2, 2020

[106]Edholm, Eric. Chiefs' insane revival against Texans joins list of biggest postseason comebacks ever. January 12, 2020

[107]Teicher, Adam. Patrick Mahomes lifts Chiefs to first Super Bowl in 50 years. January 19, 2020

[108]https://www.imdb.com/title/tt0210945/characters/nm0403652

[109]Hickman, Craig. The Oz Principle. October 1, 1998

[110]https://www.dictionary.com/browse/blind--spot?s=t

[111]https://www.dictionary.com/browse/armorbearer?s=t

[112]Ipsos and Oxford Economics. Study: A Record 768 Million U.S. Vacation Days Went Unused in '18, Opportunity Cost in the Billions. August 16, 2019

[113]Ipsos and Oxford Economics. Study: A Record 768 Million U.S. Vacation Days Went Unused in '18, Opportunity Cost in the Billions. August 16, 2019

[114]Ipsos and Oxford Economics. Study: A Record 768 Million U.S. Vacation Days Went Unused in '18, Opportunity Cost in the Billions. August 16, 2019

[115]Maxwell, John C.. How Successful People Think: Change Your Thinking, Change Your Life. June 1, 2009

[116]Maxwell, John C.. How Successful People Think: Change Your Thinking, Change Your Life. June 1, 2009

[117]Crown Copyright in UK

[118]https://www.dictionary.com/browse/replenish?s=t

[119]The *Amplified* Bible is a Literal Equivalent translation that, by using synonyms and definitions, both explains and expands the meaning of words in the text by placing amplification in parentheses, brackets, and after keywords. This unique system of translation allows the reader to more completely and clearly grasp the meaning as it was understood in the original languages. Additionally, amplifications may provide further theological, historical, and other details for a better understanding of the text. Publisher: The Lockman Foundation

[120]https://johnmaxwellteam.com/2017-grow-through-life/

[121]Maxwell, John. C.. The 15 Invaluable Laws of Growth. October 2, 2012

[122]Maxwell, John. C.. The 15 Invaluable Laws of Growth. October 2, 2012

[123]Davis, Desola. Desoladavis.com. 2019

[124]Hickman, Craig. The Oz Principle. October 1, 1998

[125]Ziglar, Zig. Better Than Good: Creating a Life You Can't Wait to Live. September 16, 2007

[126]Ziglar, Zig. Better Than Good: Creating a Life You Can't Wait to Live. September 16, 2007

[127]Ziglar, Zig. Better Than Good: Creating a Life You Can't Wait to Live. September 16, 2007

[128]Ziglar, Zig. Better Than Good: Creating a Life You Can't Wait to Live. September 16, 2007

[129]Ziglar, Zig. Better Than Good: Creating a Life You Can't Wait to Live. September 16, 2007

[130]Ziglar, Zig. Better Than Good: Creating a Life You Can't Wait to Live. September 16, 2007

[131]Ziglar, Zig. Better Than Good: Creating a Life You Can't Wait to Live. September 16, 2007

[132]Ziglar, Zig. Better Than Good: Creating a Life You Can't Wait to Live. September 16, 2007

[133]Ziglar, Zig. Better Than Good: Creating a Life You Can't Wait to Live. September 16, 2007

[134]Ziglar, Zig. Better Than Good: Creating a Life You Can't Wait to Live. September 16, 2007

[135]Ziglar, Zig. Better Than Good: Creating a Life You Can't Wait to Live. September 16, 2007

[136]Clear, James. Atomic Habits: An Easy & Proven Way to Build Habits & Break Bad Ones. October 16, 2018

[137]Scripture quotations marked NLT are taken from the *Holy Bible*, New Living Translation, copyright 1996, 2004, 2007, 2015 by Tyndale House Foundation. Used by permission of Tyndale House Publishers, Inc., Carol Stream, Illinois 60188. All rights reserved.

[138]Avengers: Age of Ultron

[139]Senge, Peter. The Fifth Discipline: The Art & Practice of The Learning Organization. March 31, 2010

[140]Senge, Peter. The Fifth Discipline: The Art & Practice of The Learning Organization. March 31, 2010

[141]Clear, James. Mental Models: Learn How to Think Better and Gain a Mental Edge. https://jamesclear.com/mental-models

[142]Senge, Peter. The Fifth Discipline: The Art & Practice of The Learning Organization. March 31, 2010

[143]Senge, Peter. The Fifth Discipline: The Art & Practice of The Learning Organization. March 31, 2010

[144]Senge, Peter. The Fifth Discipline: The Art & Practice of The Learning Organization. March 31, 2010

[145]Scripture quotations marked NLT are taken from the *Holy Bible*, New Living Translation, copyright 1996, 2004, 2007, 2015 by Tyndale House Foundation. Used by permission of Tyndale House Publishers, Inc., Carol Stream, Illinois 60188. All rights reserved.

[146]Gibson, Corey. Jesus Focused Life: Living and Leading With a Purpose. March 15, 2019

ABOUT THE AUTHOR

Jason Davis is a husband, teacher, encourager, speaker, and Stewardship Coach. By the leading of the Holy Spirit, he founded Jericho Force Enterprises in Fall 2017. He and his company provide corporate wellness programs, empowering small business owners with financial peace of mind, leadership development, and the attitude of a team player.

Jason has helped lead people out of over $310,000 of debt and put away upwards of $100,000 in savings. His impact extends to the organizational level, having trained over 1000 plus people on the concepts of leadership development and teamwork.

Jason is a John Maxwell Certified Trainer and Coach, a DISCflex Certified Coach, a graduate of Dave Ramsey's Financial Coach Master Training, and a Kanban Management Professional.